The Caledonian Games
in
Nineteenth-Century
America

The Caledonian Games in Nineteenth-Century America

Gerald Redmond

Rutherford ● Madison ● Teaneck
Fairleigh Dickinson University Press

Associated University Presses, Inc.
Cranbury, New Jersey 08512

ISBN: 0-8386-7820-3
Printed in the United States of America

To my wife, Madge,
and our sons, Paul, Philip, and Gary

Contents

Preface

This book derives from my time spent at the University of Massachusetts as a research assistant in sports history. The topic suggested itself largely because there was so little information about the Caledonian Games in the United States.

The spread of all sporting customs has an enduring fascination, but the worldwide dispersal of these Games in particular became very evident to me during the years I spent in Dunedin, New Zealand, from 1965 to 1968. This is a former Scottish settlement (the name Dunedin represents "New Edinburgh" in Gaelic), and the University of Otago there was founded in 1869. The Highland Games were a familiar aspect of the local scene before the nineteenth century ended, and there are references to such events as "pole-leaping," "the three-legged race," and "the hop, step and jump," among others. A visit to Melbourne, Australia, during this period confirmed that Scots there, too, maintained their sporting customs around that time.

Carl Diem has stated that the development of track and field athletics in England during the nineteenth century was greatly influenced by events in Scotland. Some Canadian sports historians also readily concede the Scottish origins of this sport in their country. This book is an attempt to provide more information about the Scottish Games in the United States during the nineteenth century, and to indicate their contributing influence upon the development of American track and field. I hope that it may be of some use within the much larger and continuing study of the contribution of the immigrant to North American sport in general.

I am greatly indebted to Dr. Guy M. Lewis of the University of Massachusetts for his expert advice and constant encouragement, always given with the utmost courtesy and patience. I am also grateful to the following for their interest: Drs. D. C. Bischoff, M. A. Coffey, and H. J. VanderZwaag.

I wish to thank the many archivists and reference librarians in various Colleges, Libraries, Museums, and Universities who provided me with assistance and information. I am particularly grateful to James G. Spence, Minister of the Second Presbyterian Church in New York City, for access to the documents of the New York Caledonian Club, 1867–1875, and to David Webster, Senior Technical Officer of the Scottish Council of Physical Recreation, for his contribution of illustrative material. Many officials of various Scottish associations, and individuals connected with them, have been very helpful, and to them I also extend my thanks.

Finally, my gratitude is due to my wife, who not only typed the manuscript, but made pertinent suggestions at appropriate times, which were acted upon with advantage.

G.R.

Acknowledgments

I would like to thank Harvard University Press for permission to quote from Rowland Tappan Berthoff, *British Immigrants in Industrial America*, 1953.

I am grateful to *The New York Times* for permission to quote from the obituary notice for Mr. George Goldie and from their "Special to *The New York Times*" report on his life in the issue for February 25, 1920. © by The New York Times Company. Reprinted by permission.

The Caledonian Games
in
Nineteenth-Century
America

1
Introduction

Early Scottish immigrants to the United States brought many aspects of their cultural heritage with them. In order to preserve these customs, Scottish societies of various types (e.g., Burns Society, Caledonian Club, Order of Scottish Clans, St. Andrew's Society), appeared in many parts of their adopted country. One of these customs was the traditional Highland Games, believed to be of Celtic origin. These Games were an annual affair and consisted of Scottish dancing and music, and athletic contests of various types, such as foot races, putting the heavy stone, throwing the hammer, and tossing the caber. In the United States these Games were usually referred to as "the Caledonian Games." They were sponsored mostly by the Caledonian Clubs, but other Scottish societies held games also.

The first reference to Games by a Scottish society in the United States appeared in the *Emigrant and Old Countryman*, October 19, 1836, in which a writer described the Highland Society of New York's "First Sportive Meeting" in that year. However, it is not certain that track and field athletic activities were participated in on this occasion. Most references cite traditional Games as being started by Boston Scotsmen in 1853. One refers to these same Scotsmen, however, as meeting "for several summers" beforehand "for their traditional games." After 1853, references to the Games become more frequent and informative. In the post-Civil War period, the Caledonian Games experienced their greatest era before entering a period of decline in the latter part of the nineteenth century.

During this period Scots in Boston, New York, Philadelphia, San Francisco, and several other large cities, as well as in smaller towns and rural areas, staged their Highland Games. Caledonian Clubs, for the most part, directed these patriotic field days, which included events such as throwing the hammer, putting the stone, tossing the caber, vaulting with the pole, the running high leap, the standing high leap, the long jump, the standing broad jump, the hitch and kick, the hop, step, and leap, hurdle races, the tug o'war, and foot races that varied in distance from about 100 yards to one mile. Novelty events like "sack races," "three-legged races" and "wheelbarrow races (blindfolded)" were also popular. Americans as well as their own countrymen attended by the thousands all over the country. In 1868 the New York Athletic Club was founded, and members of the New York Caledonian Club (founded 12 years earlier) competed in its first open meeting, the events of which had been part of the Caledonian Games for many years. In the previous year, 1867, international contests were held for the first time between the Caledonian Clubs of the United States and their opposite number in Canada. Three years later, Caledonian Clubs of both countries federated as the North American Caledonian Association.

Princeton, a Presbyterian College with a famous Scottish president, held its first "Caledonian Games" in 1873. These were the inspiration of George Goldie, the College's Scottish gymnastics instructor, formerly a circus performer and Caledonian Games' champion in Canada and the United States. He was also Director of Athletics for the New York Athletic Club between 1885 and 1893. The First Annual Field Meeting of the Intercollegiate American Amateur Athletic Association was held in 1876, in which Princeton successfully competed and won first place. The events had formed the major part of Princeton's annual Caledonian Games for the previous three years, and the students had the benefit of Goldie's expert guidance.

Some of the younger members of the New York Caledonian Club broke away to form the Scottish-American Athletic Club in 1875, and this became a very successful amateur club in the New York area. By 1879, there were about a hundred such clubs in this eastern part of the United States. In this year, seven clubs became charter members of the National Association of Amateur Athletes of America. The annual championship games of this Association included many Caledonian events. Dissension led to the formation of the Amateur Athletic Union of the United States in 1888, which claimed jurisdiction over amateur sport, including track and field athletics.

American Scots had first gathered in 1836 at New York to formally celebrate the sports of their native land. Before the Civil War began, Caledonian Clubs were promoting professional running, jumping, throwing, and walking events at their annual Games. In the post-Civil War period, these Games became a nationwide institution and the Clubs' primary concern. The emergence and increase in number of amateur athletic clubs that participated in track and field also came about in the post-Civil War period. Their growth culminated in the formation of a national association for their sport in 1879, and for all amateur sport in 1888. After 1869, a parallel development took place on college campuses when students formed athletic associations. Only seven years later, the Intercollegiate American Amateur Athletic Association was formed. In contrast, the Caledonian Games by 1888 were in decline. The relationship between these events is the subject of this study.

Other research on the Caledonian Games is limited. The author is aware of no other dissertation, thesis, or textbook on this topic alone. References to the Games usually occur in a narrative where the Caledonian Games are not the main concern and are usually brief; otherwise mention is usually limited to a portion of an article or chapter.

American sports historians provide little or no information pertaining to the Caledonian Games. For example, John R. Betts, "Organized Sport in Industrial America" (Ph.D. dissertation, Columbia University, 1952), devotes only three sentences, in different chapters, in a text of 754 pages. No mention at all is made in two other famous works, John A. Krout, *Annals of American Sport*, vol. 15, *The Pageant of America series*, 15 vols., (New York: United States Publishers Association), and Herbert Manchester, *Four Centuries of Sport in America*, (New York: Benjamin Blom, 1951). Also, no mention is made in the narrative of Foster Rhea Dulles, *A History of Recreation: America Learns to Play* (New York: Appleton-Century-Crofts, 1965), although an illustration of "The Great International Caledonian Games held at New York, 1867" is included.

The student of physical education who searches the histories of his subject for information pertaining to the

Caledonian Games fares a little better, although the text which is perhaps best known in this area, Deobold B. Van Dalen, Elmer D. Mitchell, and Bruce L. Bennett, *A World History of Physical Education* (Englewood Cliffs, N.J.: Prentice-Hall Inc., 1953), also makes no reference to the Caledonian Games.* Brief but significant mention is made by Fred Eugene Leonard and George B. Affleck, *The History of Physical Education* (Philadelphia: Lea and Febiger, 1947), and by Charles W. Hackensmith, *History of Physical Education* (New York: Harper and Row, 1966).

The most fertile area for information about the Caledonian Games appears to be texts of history and political science, which allude to Scottish emigration to the United States. By far the most profitable source is Rowland Tappan Berthoff, *British Immigrants in Industrial America* (Cambridge: Harvard University Press, 1953), although even this amounts only to approximately three pages. Other brief mention is found in Gordon Donaldson, *The Scots Overseas* (London: Robert Hale, 1966), and Peter Ross, *The Scot in America* (New York: The Raeburn Book Company, 1896).

Some histories of athletics, either of a general nature or of a specific institution, also provide information. Studies of this type in which the Caledonian Games are mentioned are the following: Frank Presbrey, *Athletics at Princeton: A History* (New York: Frank Presbrey Company, 1901); Augustus Maier, "Physical Training in Athletic Clubs" (thesis, Springfield College, 1904); Frederick William Janssen, *A History of American Athletics and Aquatics, 1829–1888* (New York: Outing Co. Ltd.,

* *However, three sentences are devoted to the Caledonian Games in the revised edition, 1971, just published.*

1888); Schroeder, "History of the AAU of the US" (thesis, Springfield College, 1912)[1] and Robert Korsgaard, "A History of the Amateur Athletic Union of the United States" (Ph.D. dissertation, Columbia University, 1952). Brief mention occurs also in Roberto L. Quercetani, *A World History of Track and Field Athletics, 1864–1964* (London: Oxford University Press, 1964).

The importance of the Caledonian Games in American track and field history has been evaluated differently by these authors. Some authors, mainly in sports history, afford them no place. Others, mainly in athletics or physical education history, suggest that the Games were a contributing influence to early American track and field, together with other factors. On the other hand, two authors on the history of immigration state categorically that the Caledonian Games were definitely the forerunners of American track and field athletics, and the significant influence. These latter authors have not generally discussed the possibility, as some physical education historians have done, that other factors were also influential, such as the English Universities' athletics of the time, or the appendages to the rowing regattas of the early 1870s.

The problem, then, is which, if any, is the correct evaluation of their contribution in this respect? One important fact is that none of the authors listed was writing specifically about the Caledonian Games alone, and/or with reference to their contribution to American track and field athletics.

The Caledonian Games were an important influence in the early development of track and field athletics in the United States. They were the first kind of organized track

---

1. The author's first name or initial is not indicated, nor what degree was awarded.

and field to appear on the North American continent. They were intimately connected with track and field origins in the eastern colleges and universities, and one of the latter provided the New York Athletic Club with its first Director of Athletics. A Caledonian athlete won the first intercollegiate track event in the United States. The Games regularly attracted much larger audiences, in several cities, than any other amateur athletic club was ever able to do in the same century.

Their influence, therefore, was a most significant one. A knowledge of the contribution of the Caledonian Games is essential for an understanding of the history of track and field athletics in the United States. This contribution has rarely been exaggerated, but for too long now it has been either missing or diminished.

2
Gaelic Origins
and the New World

The Highland Games originated in contests among the Scotsmen's Celtic ancestors.[1] Their activities survived the centuries and became a customary part of Scottish life. After formalization in the early nineteenth century, Scottish emigration was responsible for the dispersal of the Highland Games beyond the land of their birth, and for their appearance on the North American continent.

Britain was invaded by successive waves of Celts from about 500 B.C. They were an Alpine people, and from their overcrowded lands on the Upper Rhine and Danube they succeeded the Bronze Age Beaker Folk resident in Britain, and introduced the technology of the Iron Age. Celts were established in England, Ireland, Scotland, and Wales, where they later were driven by the Romans and Anglo-Saxons.[2]

Caledonia was the Roman name given to Scotland, and the term "Caledonian" has ever since been used to denote

---

1. John Osborne, *Britain* (Time-Life International [Nederland], N.V., 1967), pp. 26–27.

2. *The Observer*, 12 February 1967, p. 21. (A special color supplement, "Who Are the British?" by Esther Ronay).

a native of Scotland.[3] The Caledonians, from the Chief to the lowest clansman, delighted in athletic exercises and "vied with each other in generous contention, the highest individual being often the strongest and most accomplished in feats of prowess."[4] These athletic exercises were apparently participated in as a social custom:

> The clach-neart, literally stone of strength, or the putting stone, is a favorite and ancient amusement, and consists in projecting a large round stone to the greatest possible distance. It was formerly the custom to have one of these lying at the gate of every chieftain's house, and on the arrival of a stranger, he was asked as a compliment to throw. Indeed, when chiefs or gentlemen called on each other, their followers always diverted themselves in wrestling, fencing, putting, running, etc.[5]

Throwing a heavy sledge-hammer was also a popular trial of strength, and the ability to run swiftly was greatly valued, over short or long distances. So, too, was a form of running jump: "The Geal ruith, or racing game, which comprehended the running leap, to the Highlanders so useful an accomplishment, was sedulously practised, and the gilli ruith, or running footman, was capable of performing astonishing feats of pedestrianism, both in dis-

---

3. James Logan, *The Scotish [sic] Gael,* 5th American ed., (Hartford: S. Andrews and Son, 1851). The author was a Fellow of the Society of Antiquaries of Scotland.
4. *Ibid.* p. 442.
5. *Ibid.* See also *The Scottish Annual and Book of the Braemar Gathering* (Arbroath: The Herald Press, published annually 1924 to date), p. 119, hereafter referred to as *Scottish Annual;* and David Webster, *Scottish Highland Games* (Glasgow and London: Collins, 1959), p. 50; Wyness Fenton, *Royal Valley: The Story of the Aberdeenshire Dee* (Aberdeen: Alex. P. Reid & Sons, 1968), pp. 281–85.

tance and velocity."[6] The geal-ruith was the forerunner of the hop, step, and leap.[7]

There was also the clach cuid fir, or "manhood stone," weighing more than a hundredweight (112 lbs.), which a youth was required to lift and place on top of another about four feet high, before being entitled to wear the bonnet.[8] Unlike the running, jumping, putting the stone, and throwing the hammer contests, this event has not survived to modern times.

The Tailtin or Tailteann Games in Ireland preceded these Celtic pastimes in Scotland. Having originated at Telltown, County Meath, in 1829 b.c., the Games survived at least until 1168 or 1198 a.d., and consisted of running, jumping, wrestling, fencing, sham battles, chariot-racing, the gaelbolga or feat of throwing the dart, and the roth-cleas, or wheel feat, "from which has originated the practice of throwing the hammer." The "roth-cleas" was apparently a chariot wheel. The same author maintained on the next page, however, that "Scientific hammer-throwing originated, without doubt, in Scotland."[9]

Hammer-throwing may have been a Celtic pastime on both sides of the Irish Sea, but the Scots eventually formalized, popularized, and exported the event. Folklore or

---

6. Logan, p. 442.
7. *Scottish Annual* p. 119; Webster, p. 90; Fenton, pp. 284–85.
8. *Scottish Annual*, p. 119; Webster, p. 90.
9. Malcolm W. Ford, "Hammer-Throwing," *Outing*, September 1892, pp. 448–50. See also Roberto L. Quercetani, *A World History of Track and Field Athletics, 1864–1964* (London: Oxford University Press, 1964), p. xv; and Melvyn Watman, *History of British Athletics* (London: Robert Hale, 1968), p. 1. The Tailtin or Tailteann Games also preceded the Greek Olympic Games, which featured some similar events. See John Kiernan and Arthur Daley, *The Story of the Olympic Games, 776 B.C.–1960 A.D.* (Philadelphia: J. B. Lippincott Company, 1961) pp. 11–18; and E. Norman Gardiner, *Athletics of the Ancient World* (Oxford: Clarendon Press, 1967), pp. 18–229.

fact, the Tailtin Games remained rooted in their native Ireland. Their Caledonian counterpart, in contrast, enjoyed a worldwide dispersal, particularly in the nineteenth century. The clach-neart, for instance, was found to be in use centuries later, an ocean removed from its Gaelic origin:

> John D. McPherson . . . is represented here in Highland costume with a stone in his hand, for from the old-time Scotch game, putting the stone, came putting the shot; and even at this day a number of Caledonian Clubs in America give competitors a stone to put in place of an iron or lead sphere.[10]

These Celtic activities possibly lapsed during Roman and Saxon invasions, to undergo a revival afterwards through an upsurge of Scottish nationalism, when they became known as the "Highland Games."

According to tradition, the first Braemar Gathering was held under the patronage of King Malcolm Canmore in the eleventh century. There was a hill race on the Braes of Mar, quoted as the first of many Royal interests in the athletic abilities of the Scots.[11] The victor of Bannockburn, King Robert Bruce, allowed the town of Ceres, in Fife, to hold Games in commemoration of the battle. At the Games in 1332, "a heavy rock was fetched from the bed of a mountain stream, and the hammer was a huge club with an iron head."[12] The sixteenth-century English

---

10. Malcolm W. Ford, "Shot-Putting," *Outing*, July 1892, p. 287.
11. *Scottish Annual*, p. 113; Webster, pp. 12–13.
12. Carl Diem, *Weltgeschichte des Sports und der Leibeserziehung* (Stuttgart, 1960: J. G. Cotta'sche Buchhandlung Nachf, Gmb H), pp. 685–86. Webster, p. 50, mentions the surprise of an overseas visitor, who had remarked on the roundness and smoothness of the stone, when told that the best stones are quite untouched by tools: "They

chronicler, Raphael Holmshead, has described the sporting activity of the Scottish Clans of the time:

> They would not live in such security that thereby they would suffer their bodies and forces to degenerate, but they did keep themselves in their former activity and nimbleness of lives, either with continual hunting or with running from the hills unto the valleys, or from the valleys unto the hills, or with wrestling and such kind of pastimes, whereby they are never idle.[13]

Similar sporting activities were also popular far to the south of the Highlands during these centuries. In twelfth-century England open spaces were provided so that Londoners could practice "leaping, wrestling, casting of the stone, and playing with the ball."[14] Hammer-throwing, or "casting the bar," and weight-putting were known during the reigns of Edward II and Edward III. The "matrimonial monarch" himself, Henry VIII, was an all-round athlete.[15] Between his reign and the nineteenth century, when modern track and field athletics in England emerged in organized form, the British were distinctly a sports-loving people who ensured the survival of many athletic pastimes.[16] But these were largely informal affairs, of a

---

come from the river beds where the action of the water over the years has worn the stones to the very shape and texture required for shot-putters." Also, Watman, p. 1, mentions the Scottish Highland Games as dating back to the fourteenth century or earlier.

13. As quoted in *Scottish Annual*, p. 113; Fenton, pp. 281–82.

14. Watman, p. 15.

15. *Ibid.*, pp. 15–16; Ford, "Hammer Throwing," pp. 448–49; Webster, p. 45, gives an account of Henry VIII tossing the caber, which was also known at that time as "Ye casting of the Bar." So, too, does *Scottish Annual*, p. 119.

16. Diem, p. 45; Lilly C. Stone, *English Sports and Recreations* (Washington: Folger Shakespeare Library, 1960); Stonehenge, *British Rural Sports* (London: Frederick Warne & Co., 1872). "Stonehenge"

random and localized nature, with no apparent national organization, until the nineteenth century.

The previous century was a crucial period for Scotland. The early Jacobite risings ended in grief at Culloden in 1746, where more Scots fought with the Duke of Cumberland than with Bonnie Prince Charles. The cruel restrictions placed upon the "rebel Scots" afterwards, mostly Highlanders, severely curtailed all Highland customs, including the Games. "The Disarming Act of 1747 sealed the doom of every Highland Meeting, the Braemar Gathering among many others."[17] The wearing of Highland dress, including the kilt, and traditional dance and music were also banned. For nearly forty years a culture was suspended.

The revival of the old ways came with the formation of Highland Societies. In 1781 the first Society Gathering took place at Falkirk, and in 1788 the Northern Meeting was instituted at Inverness.[18] The ancient and honorable name of "Braemar" reappeared, also:

> In the year 1800, three carpenters in the Braemar district formed a provident Society called the Wright's Walk, which later became Registered and Incorporated and subsequently designated the Braemar Royal Highland Society.
> In 1832, the Society held its first Highland Games—or should we say revived the earlier Gatherings?[19]

is said to be a pseudonym for John Henry Walsh; Joseph Strutt, *The Sports and Pastimes of the People of England* (London: Thomas Tegg, 73 Cheapside, 1838); Horatio Smith, *Festivals, Games and Amusements* (New York: J and J Harper, 1831); Casper W. Whitney, *A Sporting Pilgrimage* (New York: Harper and Brothers, 1894); Norman Wymer, *Sport in England: A History of Two Thousand Years of Games and Pastimes* (London: George G. Harrap & Co. Ltd., 1949).

17. *Scottish Annual*, p. 120.
18. Webster, p. 14.
19. *Scottish Annual*, p. 120; Sir Iain Colquhoun and Hugh Machell, *Highland Gatherings* (London, 1927), pp. 61–64.

These were held on August 23, when the events were: "putting the stone, throwing the hammer, tossing the caber, running and length of service," and £5 was given in prizes for the five events (probably £1 to the winner of each event).[20] Ten years earlier at Inverness, a foot race of eight miles was run in fifty minutes.[21]

The Highland Games and Gatherings of the eighteenth and early nineteenth centuries were not merely "athletic" contests of such events as throwing the hammer, tossing the caber, and foot-races. These formed a traditional "core," certainly, but meetings were conspicuous by the extreme diversity of activities at this time. Spear-throwing, broad sword, two-handed sword and dirk competitions, archery contests, cudgel-play, wrestling, and "Best Dressed Highlander" events, as well as piping and dancing contests, took place.[22] Horse-racing for large money-prizes was a favorite pastime at Inverness in connection with the Annual Gatherings.[23] In 1835 there was "a boat race, rifle practice and pigeon shoot."[24] Lavish feasts at banquets, and elegant balls, were also a feature.[25] One peculiar event was the lifting of a huge boulder weighing more than a hundred pounds, over a bar five feet high, liable to result in "the rupture of blood-vessels or breaking of backs."[26] And a particularly grisly one was the dismembering of three cows, felled and stunned by a sledge-hammer, at a payment of five guineas a joint, which took over four hours to accomplish.[27] Most novelty events were far less barbaric than this gruesome exception, however.

20. Colquhoun and Machell, pp. 86–87; *Scottish Annual*, p. 103.
21. Colquhoun and Machell, p. 134; Webster, p. 87.
22. *Scottish Annual*, p. 113; Fenton, pp. 281–85.
23. Colquhoun and Machell, pp. 127–48.
24. *Ibid.*, p. 140.
25. *Ibid.*, p. 130.
26. *Ibid.*, p. 134; Webster, p. 87.
27. *Ibid.*

Bicycle races, greased pig chases, and shinty were some of the other "out-of-the-ordinary items" in later years.[28] An emphasis upon the traditional athletic events usually associated with the Highland Games increased, and a pattern of concentration upon these, with the addition of music and dancing, gradually evolved.

Typical of this emerging pattern were the Braemar Games of 1837, with the following events: throwing the 16 lb. hammer, throwing the 12 lb. hammer, putting the 21 lb. stone, hop, step, and leap, high leap, 250 yards, 100 yards sack race, wheelbarrow race, rifle-shooting, and wrestling. All the events had money-prizes and the victor of the latter gained "£3 and collection of 35s. as well."[29] In 1838 the sports were similar, and in 1839 "races were started for the people. The starter was Mr. Peter of Yorkshire, who had won the St. Leger three times. Hurdle races and steeplechases were added."[30] The usual social dining and dancing, and concerts, followed the proceedings. In 1841 came the introduction of a Highland piping and dancing in full costume, plus a contest for the reading and translating of the Gaelic language.[31]

The visit of Prince Albert in 1847 to the Braemar Gathering, and of Queen Victoria and her Consort a year later, began the association with the British Royal Family which continues today:

> In half an hour, there was such foot racing, hill climbing, hammer-throwing and caber tossing as only the Highlands of Scotland can produce, and none but such men as those of Braemar and Athol can perform.
> One Herculean Highlander threw a sixteen pound ham-

---

28. Webster, p. 87.
29. Colquhoun and Machell, p. 142.
30. *Ibid.*, pp. 142–43.
31. *Ibid.*, p. 143; *Scottish Annual*, p. 103.

mer ninety feet, seven inches, and five stalwart Celts ran up
Creag Coinneach, for a distance of half a mile, in from
seven to nine minutes. The foremost runner in this race
climbed the face of the hill as nimbly as a deer and accomplished this feat so cleverly that Her Majesty, who had a
view of the proceedings through a telescope, presented five
pounds for his agility.[32]

The popularity and prestige of the Games were increased
by this and succeeding Royal Visits.[33]

Similar Games were held in other parts of Scotland as
well, and Lowlanders and Borderers often disputed the
asserted superiority of the Highlanders.[34] At the Innerleithen Border Games on August 10, 1835, the events
were: running hop, step, and leap; standing hop, step,
and leap; putting the 22 lb. ball; putting the 16 lb. ball;
and throwing the 15 lb. hammer. The first two events also
featured in the Galashiels Games in July, 1841, plus the
running leap and the hitch and kick. "Vaulting with the
pole," won at a height of 8 feet 4 inches, was an event in
the Edinburgh Games in July, 1850. In the same month
of the same year Highland Games even appeared in London at the Scottish Fete held in Lord Holland's Park.[35]

In time there was hardly a district in Scotland where
the Games had not taken place. Besides the places already
mentioned, the athletic events appeared in Aboyne, Ari-
saig, Ballater, Banchory, Banff, Cowal, Dyce, Glenisla,

32. *Scottish Annual,* p. 107.
33. Webster, p. 14.
34. *Ibid.; Scottish-American Journal,* November 21, 1868, p. 2. The
Scots in Ulster, Northern Ireland, also participated in "boxing matches,
wrestling, foot races, and other athletic exercises." See Edward L.
Parker," *History of Londonderry,* as quoted in Henry Jones Ford, *The
Scotch-Irish in America* (New York: Peter Smith, 1941), pp. 239–43.
35. *Scottish-American Journal,* November 21, 1868, p. 2.

Invergordon, Lonach, Luss, Oban, Pitlochry, Tarland, Tobermory, and Tuniff. Games were held elsewhere also.[36] Despite the addition and discarding of novelty events at various times, "the heavy athletics, together with dancing and piping will always form 95% of the programme at a Gathering."[37] A "standard" program consisted of: highland dancing and music, tossing the caber, putting the light and heavy stone, throwing the light and heavy hammer, throwing the 28-lb. and 56-lb. weight, wrestling, pole-vaulting, hill races, novelty events such as the sack race, three-legged race, wheelbarrow race, and greased pig chases, tug-o'war, running events and hurdle races over various distances, standing high and long jumps, running high and long jumps, and the hop, step, and jump.

Money-prizes and other rewards were always an incentive to compete well and often, if this was needed. Many of the best performers toured the different Games and used their physical talents for financial reward. On at least one occasion the athletes went on strike for better cash prizes.[38] Another time, however, a champion performed without payment.[39] Undoubtedly there was a mercenary element in the Games, but there was an evident pride in performance also, which often transcended professional inducements.

But any success the Games achieved in their native land before 1860 was about to be surpassed. Brother Scots had carried their customs with them to the New World in previous years. Indeed, many were emigrating still. In America and Canada these pastimes flourished in their new en-

---

36. Webster, pp. 9–155; Francis Drake Carnell, *It's An Old Scottish Custom* (London: Peter Davies, 1939), pp. 218–19.
37. Webster, p. 88.
38. *Ibid.*, p. 103.
39. *Ibid.*, p. 100.

vironment also. The processes of increasing immigration, industrialization, and urbanization on the new continent accelerated their growth. The Games obtained an American arena and audience which the much smaller and far less-populated Scotland could never match. One visiting Scottish Champion athlete, "feted and honoured like a king," was able to earn over seven hundred dollars in a day.[40]

Since 1607 emigrants have departed from the Old World to become immigrants in the New.[41] The Scots soon became a part of this movement. They appeared in Newfoundland as early as 1620, and in East New Jersey in 1683.[42] Scottish prisoners had been deported to America and other countries in the intervening years, beginning in 1648 or 1649.[43] Emigration, both compulsory and voluntary, increased in years to come. In fact, one of Scotland's outstanding characteristics is the way in which it has regularly contributed to the population of many countries all over the world:

> The history of the Scottish nation has for many centuries now been something more than the history of the inhabitants of the geographical bounds of a small, poor and remote country. A study of spectacular outward movement of people from Scotland is part of Scottish history, in the sense that the vitality which stimulated the expansion of the nation arose from conditions within Scotland itself.[44]

These conditions varied, and reasons for emigration varied

---

40. Webster, pp. 97–98.
41. Rowland Tappan Berthoff, *British Immigrants in Industrial America* (Cambridge: Harvard University Press, 1953), p. 15.
42. Gordon Donaldson, *The Scots Overseas* (London: Robert Hale, 1966), pp. 33–36.
43. *Ibid.*, p. 38–39.
44. *Ibid.*, preface.

with them. Political or religious oppression drove many to seek tolerance elsewhere, while others were transported to America as convicts or slaves.[45] By far the most consistent and urgent reasons for emigration from Scotland, however, were the economic changes and forces which transformed the character of the country in the eighteenth and nineteenth centuries.[46] Thousands of Scots left their homeland and settled in America and other countries during this period.

Not all the immigrants of Scottish descent in the United States came from Scotland itself. From 1606 onwards Scots had settled in Ulster, Northern Ireland.[47] Before the seventeenth century had ended, many of them had made a second migration to America or Canada.[48] This process increased in the eighteenth and nineteenth centuries, mainly for familiar reasons: "Ulster emigration upon any important scale is to be attributed to economic and not to religious causes."[49] In the United States, these Ulster Scots were termed the "Scotch-Irish." They settled in many parts of the country, although Pennsylvania became the chief "Scotch-Irish centre."[50] In short, the American Scot came from Scotland and Ulster, and immigration figures included both as persons of Scottish descent.[51]

The total Scottish migration to America for the years 1763 to 1765 was estimated as high as 25,000 when "there

---

45. *Ibid.*, pp. 57–58; Berthoff, p. 15.
46. Donaldson, pp. 57–102; Marcus L. Hansen, *Atlantic Migration 1607–1860* (Cambridge: Harvard University Press, 1940), p. 120. See also John Prebble, *The Highland Clearances* (New York: Penguin Books, 1969).
47. Donaldson, p. 29–30, 107–8; Henry Jones Ford, *The Scotch-Irish in America* (New York: Peter Smith, 1941), pp. 2–41.
48. Ford, pp. 165–208; Charles A. Hanna, *The Scotch-Irish 2* (New York and London: G. P. Putnam's Sons, 1902): 6–15.
49. Ford, pp. 167–68.
50. *Ibid.*, pp. 260–90; Hanna, pp. 60–93.
51. Berthoff, pp. 1–11.

was a trickle of Scots into all the colonies."[52] They had established St. Andrew's Societies in Charlestown (1729), Philadelphia (1749), New York (1756), and Savannah (after 1750). The most important areas of settlement were Cape Fear Valley in North Carolina, the Mohawk and Upper Hudson Valleys in New York, and Altamaha Valley in Georgia.[53] In 1790 it was estimated that eight percent of the population was directly Scottish, and six percent "Scotch-Irish."[54] As America expanded rapidly westward in the next century, "a considerable contribution to this development was made by Scots . . . making a secondary migration from the coastal states."[55] Of three and a half million British immigrants who arrived in the United States between 1820 and 1870, over two percent were Scots.[56] Although a minority group, and usually outnumbered by the German or Irish in the large cities, people of Scottish descent were likely to be found anywhere in America prior to 1850.[57]

The national organizations of the American Scot were numerous, particularly in the cities, and their names all directly pertained to Scotland. Philadelphia had a St. Andrew's Society, a Burns Club, a Caledonian Club, and Scots' Thistle Society before the Civil War.[58] New York

---

52. Donaldson, p. 104.
53. *Ibid.*; Peter Benedict Sheridan, Jr., "The Immigrant in Philadelphia, 1827–1860" (Ph. D. dissertation, Georgetown University, 1957), pp. 53–54. The latter author gives the founding date of the St. Andrew's Society of Philadelphia as 1747.
54. Berthoff, pp. 4–5.
55. Donaldson, p. 111. See also Thomas D. Clark, *Frontier America* (New York: Charles Scribner's Sons, 1959), pp. 87–88.
56. Berthoff, pp. 5–6.
57. Donaldson, pp. 112-28; Oscar Handlin, *Boston's Immigrants: A Study in Acculturation* (Cambridge: Harvard University Press, 1959), pp. 155–56.
58. Sheridan, pp. 53–54, 76.

also had these, and others, by 1890.[59] Membership was open to persons of Scottish birth or descent.[60] The Scots who belonged to these organizations would have agreed with the sentiment that "among immigrant groups fraternal orders assisted individuals to hold fast to their native culture and helped to satisfy the nostalgic longings of strangers in a foreign land."[61] Before the nineteenth century ended, an aspect of "their native culture" affected the origin and development of a new sport in that "foreign land."

59. John L. Wilson, "The Foreign Element in New York City—IV, The Scotch," *Harper's Weekly*, June 28, 1890, pp. 513–16.

60. *Ibid.*

61. Ralph Henry Gabriel, *The Course of American Democratic Thought* (New York: The Ronald Press Company, 1940), p. 190.

3
The "First Sportive Meeting" and Others

The first replica of the Scottish Highland Games appeared in the United States during the second quarter of the nineteenth century. The first Scottish settlements were necessarily on the East Coast, near ports of landing, and the Games originated here before spreading westward later. Scots in Boston and New York led the way in successfully pioneering their traditional sports, which were favorably reported by the press. They set the example for Scots elsewhere to follow, until the Civil War limited further progress.

The first Caledonian Club was organized in Boston on March 19, 1853, and its earliest Games were held later in the same year.[1] However, this important event was preceded by some informal Scottish sporting activity, as a few Boston Scotsmen had met for their traditional Games "for several summers" previously.[2] Certainly the Boston

1. Fred Eugene Leonard and George B. Affleck, *History of Physical Education* (Philadelphia: Lea and Febiger, 1947), p. 282; Oscar Handlin, *Boston's Immigrants: A Study in Acculturation* (Cambridge: Harvard University Press, 1959), pp. 155–56.

2. Rowland Tappan Berthoff, *British Immigrants in Industrial America* (Cambridge: Harvard University Press, 1953) p. 167. The author is quoting from the *"Boston Scotsman,* April 7, 1906, and February 16, 1907," and gives the source location as The Order of Scottish Clans, Boston. However, officials of this organization say they do not have this

Caledonians were socially active before this, as "the Seventh Annual Caledonian Ball" was held on the evening of March 18, 1853, at Union Hall.[3] The first Ball presumably took place in 1847.

Over ten years earlier, in the New York area, the Scots were also active in a social and sporting fashion. The Highland Society of New York held its "first Sportive Meeting" in 1836, "to renew the Sports of their Native Land" at the Elysian Fields in Hoboken.[4] The activities seem to have been confined to games of caman, or shinty, followed by dancing accompanied by the bagpipes, but it represented an expression of Scottish patriotic feeling, held with all the native pageantry the participants could muster.

The Chief marshalled the Clans opposite Burns House. In front were two blue flags bearing the cross of St. Andrew, patron Saint of Scotland, "each surmounted by a Lochaber axe, displayed in the firm grasp of two sturdy sons of the Gael."[5] The Chief himself was attired in green tartan, equipped with shield, claymore, dirk, and pistol, and wearing a bonnet topped with three eagle feathers. Behind him came three Pipers. Next came the assembly dressed in Highland costume, including a resplendent Deputy Chieftain. This "Celtic band" marched to the sports field and was cheered by the spectators on arrival. After the first few games "the Society proceeded to the Elysian cottage, where they partook of a Co'd Collation"

paper in their possession. Further efforts to locate it in periodical guides, Boston libraries, and the Library of Congress, Washington, D.C., have been unsuccessful. The last named is circulating a request in an attempt to determine the existence and location of the source.

3. *Boston Post*, March 18, 1853, p. 2; *Boston Daily Evening Transcript*, March 19, 1853, p. 2.

4. *Emigrant and Old Countryman*, October 19, 1836; Berthoff, p. 151.

5. *Emigrant and Old Countryman*, October 19, 1836.

before returning to the sports. When these ended, they paraded back to Burns House where another crowd awaited their return, stopping en route only to partake again, this time of "their native mountain dew, and Oaten Cake."[6]

Although the other traditional Highland athletic activities do not appear to have formed a part of the program, this event was important. Scotsmen had gathered for the main (if not the only) purpose of participating in traditional sporting activity in their adopted land. Also, the initial marshalling, the parade with bagpipes to the appointed arena, the sports and refreshments, and the concluding dancing and revelry, set a pattern for the more comprehensive meetings which were destined to follow. The Scots were also parading in Clan tartans at Philadelphia in 1838, to the tune of "The Campbells are coming."[7]

Such sights became frequent in succeeding years, organized by a number of Scottish societies to celebrate various national customs. The largest and most consistent audiences of all patronized the annual sports held by the Caledonian Clubs. The Games of these clubs were eventually witnessed in well over a hundred major cities and towns across America.[8]

A reporter for the *Boston Daily Globe* of August 29, 1879, has described the origin and success of the oldest Club with evident pride:

> The Boston Caledonian Club held their twenty-sixth annual picnic and athletic entertainment at Spy Pond grove

6. *Ibid.*
7. Peter Benedict Sheridan, "The Immigrant in Philadelphia," (Ph. D. dissertation, Georgetown University, 1957), p. 56.
8. Berthoff, pp. 167–70.

yesterday. Nature smiled upon the athletes, and a more perfect day could not have been selected for out-door sports. There are many facts in the history of this club that give it a special interest to Caledonians. In this city the movement had its inception in the early part of 1853; circulars were extensively distributed amongst the Scottish residents of Boston and vicinity, announcing a meeting to be held in the Merchants' Exchange of this city, for the purpose of considering the advisability of organizing a Caledonian club. The meeting was held, and Mr. A. W. Wilson was appointed chairman, and announced the purpose for which the meeting was called. A number of gentlemen delivered addresses, and spoke strongly in favor of organizing a Caledonian club, for the purpose of perpetuating "the manners and customs, literature, the Highland costume and the athletic games of Scotland, as practised by our forefathers." On the voice of the meeting being taken, it was unanimously voted that the gentlemen here present themselves under the name and title of "The Boston Caledonian Club." The following were elected officers for the year 1853–4: Chief: A. W. Wilson; first Chieftain, J. Anderson; second Chieftain, Peter Donald; henchman (secretary), John Patterson. Thus, in Boston was established the first Caledonian club on this continent. Since then this club had assisted in the foundations and formation of nearly every Caledonian club in this country. It is the parent and originator of all athletic sports that have now become so popular over this continent.[9]

The traditional Games were not the only concern of the Caledonian Clubs. As time went by, however, the phenomenal success of the Caledonian Games of these clubs diminished other obligations, and the Games became the greatest source of revenue for most clubs. Besides, other

---

9. *Boston Daily Globe,* August 29, 1879, p. 4.

Scottish Societies existed whose main considerations were for the preservation of Scottish literature and other customs. As early as 1859, for example, Philadelphia had a St. Andrew's Society, Burns Club, and a Scots' Thistle Society, as well as a Caledonian Club.[10]

The parent Club's first offspring appeared three years later in 1856, and in New York, where the Highland Society had held its "first Sportive Meeting" some twenty years before.[11] The New York Caledonian Club held its first Games in 1857.[12] In the following year, the Club advertised its Games beforehand, indicating an admission charge of twenty-five cents.[13] This enterprise became a regular policy of the Caledonian Clubs and contributed to the success of their Games. In years to come, similar and bigger advertisements were placed in more newspapers and periodicals and helped to draw the crowds.

But if the advertisement was significant, the editorial which accompanied it was even more so. The writer stated:

> We refer with pleasure to an advertisement in our Columns, announcing the occasion of the Second Annual Meeting of the New York Caledonian Club, and their performance of athletic sports. These are the kind of manly pastimes that give not only health and vigor to the frame, but place a large share of contentment in the mind, and make men fond of the soil on which they are enjoyed. Nothing cultivates patriotism so much as happiness; and

---

10. Sheridan, pp. 53–54, 76.
11. Robert Ernst, *Immigrant Life in New York City* (New York: King's Crown Press, Columbia University, 1949), p. 129; Schroeder, "History of the AAU of the US" (thesis, Springfield College, 1912), p. 1.
12. Robert Korsgaard, "A History of the Amateur Athletic Union of the United States" (Ph.D. dissertation, Columbia University, 1952), p. 22.
13. *Porter's Spirit of the Times,* September 4, 1858, p. 1.

such athletic sports as have been inaugurated here by the New York Caledonian Club are wiser than Statesmanship, and more wholesome to the heart than preacher's prayers. The New York Caledonian Club hold their high festival at Jones' Wood (Avenue A, between 68th and 69th streets, New York) on the 23rd instant.[14]

With such a testimonial the Games were off to an excellent start. The New York Caledonian Club later raised its admission price to fifty cents, attracted crowds of more than 25,000 people, and became one of the most successful of all the Caledonian Clubs.

An account of these 1858 New York Games, under the heading "Scottish Sports," described the events as throwing the heavy hammer, throwing the light hammer, putting the light stone, putting the heavy stone, tossing the caber, wheelbarrow race (blindfolded), sack race, standing high jump, running long jump, running high leap, short race, and broadsword dance.[15] An "Alex Innes" threw both hammers the greatest distances, but refused to compete for the money prizes. He might have been the first amateur athlete to compete in a field event at an organized meeting in the United States, for this was ten years before the first American amateur athletic club, which participated in track and field, was formed.

The Philadelphia Society held its first Caledonian Games in 1858, also, and they began in Newark three years later.[16] Then, although the Games continued during the conflict, further expansion was limited by the Civil War. Afterwards, the Caledonians entered an era of expansion and even greater influence.

14. *Ibid.*
15. *Ibid.*, October 2, 1858, p. 69.
16. *Ibid.*, August 14, 1869, p. 402; *Scottish-Ameircan Journal,* June 29, p. 5; Korsgaard, p. 22.

4
The Post-Civil War Period

The annual Games of the Caledonian Clubs were especially popular for at least 15 years following the Civil War.[1] The earlier clubs had shown the way and Scots elsewhere in the United States were not slow to respond. Neither was the vast American public, whose consistent patronage contributed to the popularity and success of the Caledonian Games during this period. The number of Caledonian Clubs increased until they, and the Games associated with them, became a nationwide institution. Events were increased in number and type, and the prizes in value. An affinity existed between the first amateur athletic club to be formed for track and field purposes in the United States, and the Caledonian Club in the same city. One of the foremost amateur athletic clubs was formed by the younger members of the latter. The most famous Caledonian athlete in the United States began his influential career in this period, also. Canadian Caledonian athletes competed regularly in the United States, and three years after the first International Games were held in New York, Caledonian Clubs of both countries federated in an Association. The champion athletes of Scotland came over for profitable tours of the Games in both

1. Fred Eugene Leonard and George B. Affleck, *History of Physical Education* (Philadelphia: Lea and Febiger, 1947), p. 282.

countries. Other famous visitors also attended. Entrepreneurs, gamblers, soldiers, and youngsters were among the many who delighted in the American version of the Scottish Highland Games at this time. In short, the period from the end of the Civil War to at least 1879 represented the greatest era of the Caledonian Games.

The Brooklyn Caledonian Club was organized on March 9, 1866, and held its first Games the following year.[2] Also in 1867, the St. Andrew's Society of Milwaukee, Wisconsin, held the first of its annual Games.[3] At the Ninth Annual Games of the Newark Caledonian Club in 1869, there were delegations from "New York, Germantown, Brooklyn, Philadelphia, and other large cities."[4] Another commendation was accorded to the athletic and industrious Scotsmen:

> These Caledonian Games are growing more popular every year, and the great success which has attended those given heretofore by the New York Club, at Jones' Wood, testifies how they are appreciated by the public.[5]

The writer also stated that Games had already taken place that year in San Francisco, Cincinnati, Chicago, Detroit, Milwaukee, Cleveland, and Pittston. Before 1870, therefore, the Caledonian Games were already a nationwide institution, and the pace did not slacken in the seventies.

The first Annual New Haven Games began in 1871, the year in which Hudson County held its first Games.[6] The following year the Syracuse Caledonian Club, New

2. *New York Times,* August 18, p. 6; August 11, 1874, p. 8; *Scottish-American Journal,* July 23, 1885, p. 5.
3. *Scottish-American Journal,* July 23, 1885, p. 5.
4. *Spirit of the Times,* August 14, 1869, p. 402.
5. *Ibid.*
6. *Scottish-American Journal,* June 25, 1874, p. 5; June 29, 1882, p. 5.

York, began its first Annual Games.[7] In 1873, the Richmond Caledonian Club of Virginia also started Games.[8] Next year Baltimore joined in the promotion.[9] A delegation from the "Scranton Caledonian Club" visited the New Haven Games in 1874, besides holding its own Games.[10] Two years later, the Norwich Caledonian Club of Connecticut held the first of its Annual Games.[11] The San Francisco Club was not alone on the West Coast, for

on the 6th inst., the third annual games of the Caledonian Club of Stockton, Cal., came off at Good Water Grove, and attracted almost all the Scots of the San Joaquin Valley. Among visitors the San Francisco CC was represented, and the Sacramento Club was represented.[12]

Between 1880, when Stockton began, and 1885, Games were initiated by Caledonian Clubs in Cleveland (Ohio), Holyoke (Massachusetts), Lake Linden (Michigan), Minneapolis (Minnesota), and Rochester and Yonkers (New York).[13] Among St. Andrews Societies, those in Buffalo and Minneapolis also held Scottish games.[14] By 1885, Caledonian Games were annual affairs in Fall River (Massachusetts), Hartford (Connecticut), Paterson (New Jersey), Providence (Rhode Island), Schenectady and Troy (New York), Washington, D.C., and many other

7. *Ibid.*, September 9, 1885, p. 8.
8. *Ibid.*, September 22, 1881, p. 8. The ninth Annual Games, and probably earlier ones, were held at West Point.
9. *Ibid.*, June 15, 1882, p. 8.
10. *Ibid.*, June 25, 1874, p. 5; July 14, 1881, p. 8.
11. *Ibid.*, July 14, 1881, p. 8.
12. *Ibid.*, May 15, 1882, p. 8.
13. *Ibid.*, July 7, 1881, p. 8; July 21, 1881, p. 8; September 8, 1881, p. 8; June 8, 1882, p. 8; September 9, 1885, p. 8; August 1, 1888, p. 8.
14. *Ibid.*, July 23, 1885, p. 5; June 29, 1882, p. 5; July 14, 1881, p. 8.

places.[15] Even the Burns Club of Fishkill, New York, held its annual Games.[16] Enthusiasm prevailed to the extent that, in 1887, it could be recorded in the *Scottish-American Journal* that "A Caledonian Club has been organized at Great Falls, Montana, with a membership of 37 enthusiastic Scots."[17] By the time another thirty years had passed, Scottish Clubs "had held games in more than 125 towns and cities."[18]

This spread of the Caledonian Games was part of the phenomenal "rise of sport" which occurred in the United States during the latter part of the nineteenth century, when the spectator period gave way to an era of participation in many sports. Immigration, industrialization and urbanization, the technological revolution, the closing of the frontier, the establishment of new values, and the status that high society gave to sport were all contributing factors.[19] The former applied mostly to the Caledonians. Immigration from the native land provided the

15. *Ibid.*, July 14, 1881, p. 8; September 9, 1885, p. 8; July 7, 1881, p. 8; *Boston Daily Globe*, August 28, 1874, p. 5; August 30, 1878, p. 2; August 29, 1884, p. 4; Thomas Wentworth Higginson, "A Day of Scottish Games," *Scribner's*, January, 1872, pp. 329–36.

16. *Scottish-American Journal*, May 18, 1882, p. 5.

17. *Ibid.*, October 5, 1887, p. 8.

18. Rowland Tappan Berthoff, *British Immigrants in Industrial America* (Cambridge: Harvard University Press, 1953), p. 167.

19. Frederic L. Paxson, "The Rise of Sport," *Mississippi Valley Historical Review* 4, September 1917: 143–68; John L. Krout, "Some Reflections on the Rise of Sport," *Proceedings of the Association of History Teachers of Middle States and Maryland* 26, May 1928: 84–93; John R. Betts, "The Technological Revolution and the Rise of Sport," *Mississippi Valley Historical Review* 40, September 1953: 231–56; and "Organized Sport in Industrial America" (Ph.D. dissertation, University of Michigan, 1951); Foster R. Dulles, *A History of Recreation: America Learns to Play* (New York: Appleton-Century-Crofts, 1965); Max Lerner, *America as a Civilization* (New York: Simon and Schuster Co., 1957), pp. 813–14; Arthur C. Cole, "Our Sporting Grandfathers," *Atlantic Monthly*, July, 1932, pp. 88–96.

members of the Caledonian Clubs, and other Scottish societies. Most of these were situated in the cities, where industry employed large numbers of immigrants.[20] Like everyone else living in the United States at the time, the Caledonians also benefited from the improvements in road and rail communications and transport, and these factors aided their progress. It became easier and quicker for athletes and spectators to attend the Games in their own locality, and in other areas as well.

The 13 pre-War events of the New York Caledonian Club had increased to 21 in 1865. At the Club's ninth anniversary Games the events were: putting the heavy stone, putting the light stone, throwing the heavy hammer, throwing the light hammer, the running jump, the standing jump, the Highland Fling, the short race, the running high leap, the boys' race, vaulting with the pole, the long race, tossing the caber, the broadsword dance, the sack race, the standing high leap, the hitch and kick, the hurdle race, the boys' hurdle race, the hop, step and jump, and the wheelbarrow race.[21] This program became typical of many throughout the land, which usually ranged from about 15 events to 25.

The heavy stone usually weighed from 22 to 24 lbs., rested on the palm of the hand, and delivered from the shoulder, with no more than five feet allowed for the run or hop beforehand (Figure 1). The light stone weighed from 16 to 18 lbs. The heavy hammer weighed from 16 to 22 lbs., and the light hammer from 12 to 16 lbs. (Figure 1). The running jump was like the broad jump of today, and the standing jump was a standing broad jump. The Highland Fling was, and is, the best known of all Scottish dances (Figure 1).

20. Berthoff, pp. 15–142.
21. New York Times, September 8, 1865, p. 2.

A large ring of over 500 feet in circumference was roped off as the arena in which the Games took place, and the short race was one lap around the ring, a distance of from 200 to 300 yards. The running high leap was akin to the high jump of today. Boys' races could be once across the ring, or one lap, depending upon the age limits. Vaulting with the pole graduated to perhaps the most spectacular field event of all, the pole-vault. The long race was two or three laps of the ring.

Tossing the caber was the most peculiarly Scottish of all the athletic events, and unlike the others, was destined to remain so. A wooden log from ten to 18 feet long, weighing between 70 and 100 lbs., was carried to the line by its thinner end. Then the athlete hurled it so that it landed on its heavier end before falling. A good "toss" made the caber fall straight forward, although sometimes it would land more sideways (Figure 2). The broadsword dance was another traditional Scottish favorite, performed over crossed swords on the ground. The sack race was a popular comedy event. Contestants had to race in sacks which completely covered their bodies, leaving nothing but their heads exposed. The usual distance was across the ring and back or once around the ring (Figure 1). The writer of one unusual account of "a very amusing sack-race" stated "In this shape they had to run an eighth of a mile and jump three hurdles."[22] The standing high leap was simply a standing high jump. In the hitch and kick, contestants had to jump, kick at a tambourine suspended at increasing heights, and land on the same foot. The hurdle race was usually twice around the ring, and the number of hurdles varied from three to eight. Five feet was the most common height of a hurdle and runners usually scrambled over them. The hop, step, and jump

22. *Ibid.*, September 3, 1880, p. 3.

was also described occasionally as the "hop, skip and jump" and was the forerunner of the triple jumps today. The wheelbarrow race was another comic event like the sack race, usually over the same distance(s). But the competitors were generally blindfolded, causing amusing (for the spectators) collisions of the heavy wooden wheelbarrows (Figure 1). A third novelty favorite was the three-legged race, where the right leg of one man was tied to the left leg of his partner, and holding each other around the waist, they raced together for the finishing line.

The large audiences which attended the Caledonian Games found plenty to amuse them. Although the athletic events formed the major part of the program, the Scotsmen responsible believed, like their forefathers, in variety and fun. Besides the events already mentioned, there were also other Scottish favorites like "the best dressed Highlander," a bagpipe competition, quoits, or Scottish-style wrestling.[23] In addition to the usual novelty events, there were also egg races and potato races.[24] In 1876, an "Old Man's Race" of 220 yards took place.[25] Ten years later a ladies' race of the same distance "excited immense enthusiasm, and the ropes were broken down in several places by the eagerness of the crowd to get a good view."[26] Throwing the 56-lb. weight was not an uncommon event, but on one occasion four men tried their strength at putting a shot weighing 56 lbs. A usual 16-lb. shot event

23. *Ibid.*, September 6, 1878, p. 3; September 4, 1885, p. 8; July 6, 1886, p. 8; Robert Korsgaard, "A History of the Amateur Athletic Union of the United States" (Ph.D. dissertation, Columbia University, 1952), p. 25.

24. *New York Times*, August 11, 1874, p. 8; July 6, 1886, p. 8; Korsgaard, p. 25.

25. *New York Times*, September 8, 1876, p. 8.

26. *Ibid.*, July 6, 1886, p. 8.

was also on the program.[27] The Caledonians were not beyond laying aside their Highland costume, putting on sailors' clothes, and dancing the sailor's hornpipe for money prizes.[28] A tug o' war between married men and single men was held at the Boston Games of 1884. The latter won in two straight heats.[29] A novelty event "caused as much fun among the spectators as confusion among the competitors." This was consistent with Caledonian policy.

The Caledonians were also assiduous in their efforts to provide activities for youngsters during their Games. Most events were naturally for adult competitors, but some were included for the younger members on most occasions. The most usual were boys' races and boys' hurdle races.[30] Age limits were a common feature of such races, ranging from "under ten" to "under sixteen," and most were "for members' sons only."[31] Boys in this category even had their own meetings:

In the early 1870's Junior Caledonian Games were held for the sons of club members. Fewer events were held than in the regular games and since the games were generally restricted to boys under 16 yrs. of age, the prizes were "useful and instructive books, with a silver medal to the contestants who carried away the greatest number of prizes."[32]

In the 1880s, a novel feature was the introduction of a

27. *Ibid.*, July 28, 1880, p. 3.
28. *Ibid.*, July 6, 1886, p. 8.
29. *Boston Daily Globe*, August 29, 1884, p. 4.
30. *New York Times*, September 8, 1865, p. 2; *Boston Daily Globe*, August 29, 1873, p. 8; August 28, 1874, p. 5.
31. *Boston Daily Globe*, August 29, 1873, p. 8; August 28, 1874, p. 5; *New York Times*, August 11, 1874, p. 8; September 4, 1874, p. 8; July 29, 1876, p. 8.
32. Korsgaard, p. 27.

drum and fife corps of youngsters, when "drum-major Eddy Morriss, 8 yrs. old, led them around the ground twice, while they played Auld Lang Syne with ear-piercing distractness."[33]

Their concern for young people also revealed itself earlier outside the Games, to the schoolchildren of Randall's Island in 1867. The Caledonian Club of New York, "anxious to encourage the boys of Randall's Island in their fondness for Scottish games and other athletic sports," visited the school and witnessed races of 300 yards and 600 yards; a hop, skip, and jump; putting the stone; and a running race for girls (Figure 3). Prizes were distributed and the Caledonians returned well-pleased with what they had seen.[34] They obviously considered it important to inculcate their sports at an early age, and this policy helped to ensure its perpetuation.

Less than a year after this visit to Randall's Island there occurred an event of great significance in the history of American track and field athletics: the founding of the New York Athletic Club:

> On a rainy September day in 1868, William B. Curtis, John C. Babcock and Henry E. Buermeyer sat in a New York rooming house discussing the zeal with which the British were turning to athletics as a means of recreation. Out of their conversation came a decision to organize an athletic club for the purpose of promoting interest in track and field events in the United States.[35]

---

33. *New York Times*, September 2, 1887, p. 3.

34. *Harper's Weekly*, November 2, 1867, p. 687.

35. John Allen Krout. *Annals of American Sport* 15, *The Pageant of America Series*, 15 vols. (New York: United States Publishers' Association, 1929): 186. The exact date of the "rainy September day" is uncertain. Schroeder, "History of the AAU of the US" (thesis, Spring-

This important meeting was preceded by the Twelfth Annual Meeting of the New York Caledonian Club, held on September 3, 1868, at Jones' Wood. This "institution that our citizens patronize liberally, and flock to in large numbers to witness the celebration of the sports of their forefathers by the Americanized Highlander, dressed out in his national costume," attracted between four and ten thousand spectators in inclement weather on that day.[36] Judges came from Boston and Montreal, and one was a champion pedestrian. The most successful competitor was a Canadian, in a program which included: putting the heavy stone (Figure 4), putting the light stone, the standing jump, throwing the heavy hammer, throwing the light hammer, the running jump, the broadsword dance, the running high jump, the short race, the boys' race (under 12), the three-legged race, vaulting with the pole, the long race, tossing the caber, walking match (eight times round, one mile), long race (one mile), the highland fling, the sack race, the standing high leap, the hitch and kick, the hurdle race (twice round over 6 hurdles), the boys' hurdle race, hop, step, and jump, and the wheelbarrow race (blindfolded).[37]

Whatever the topic of conversation of the athletically minded trio, they were not unaware of these popular Scottish athletic sports, not far removed from their meeting place. British athletics may well have been in their

---

field College, 1912) p. 3, suggests June 17, 1866, as the founding date but 1868 is the usual year given. The exact date has been presented as "September 6," "September 8," or "September 18." See Augustus Maier, "Physical Training in Athletic Clubs" (thesis, Springfield College, 1904), pp. 12, 35; S. Conant Foster, "The New York Athletic Club," *Outing*, September 1864, p. 403; Charles P. Sawyer, "Amateur Track and Field Athletics," *Scribner's*, June 1890, p. 775.

36. *New York Times*, September 4, 1868, p. 8.
37. *Ibid.*

thoughts, but their subsequent actions showed a strong Caledonian influence.

Certainly the New York Caledonian Club members were made aware of the appearance of a new club in the city that would be devoting its energies to similar athletic pastimes. At the quarterly meeting of the club, held on November 10, 1868,

> Chieftain (John) Goldie here stated for the information of the club that a new club had been formed called the N. Y. Athletic Club and hoped that the members would attend their first Games.[38]

His wish was realized. At these "first Games" of the New York Athletic Club, held at the Empire City Skating Rink on November 11, 1868, athletes from the New York Caledonian Club also competed.[39] An authority on athletics has stated that the New York Athletic Club took the initiative regarding the Caledonians' participation:

> . . . but a special invitation, or rather a challenge, was extended to the New York Caledonian Club, then, as now, the most prominent of American Caledonian Societies, and their most eminent athletes were present to compete, thus making the affair an International Match—America against Scotland. The result was, as might have been foreseen, America won the running and walking contests, while Scotland was successful with the hammer and shot and in pole-leaping, standing high jump and running long jump,—the games most common at Caledonian meetings.[40]

---

38. *Minutes of the Quarterly Meeting, New York Caledonian Club,* November 10, 1868.

39. *Scottish-American Journal,* November 21, 1868, p. 5; Sawyer, "Amateur Track and Field Athletics," *Scribner's,* June 1890, p. 775; Maier, "Physical Training in Athletic Clubs," p. 13.

40. Frederick William Janssen, *A History of American Athletics and Aquatics, 1829–1888* (New York: Outing Co. Ltd., 1888), p. 126.

In fact, running and walking events were common at Caledonian meetings, also. The fact that the events were common to the Caledonian Games, included handicaps, and were open to all, justifies the statement that the New York Athletic Club started "handicap Scottish Games" in 1868.[41] Handicaps were still a feature of amateur athletic clubs' meetings in later years.[42] Whether invited or challenged, or neither, the Caledonians were definitely successful competitors at this important meeting.

One of the most interesting Caledonians, who was later employed by this athletic club, was George Goldie. Born at Edinburgh, the capital city of Scotland, in 1841, he came to New York and was employed in business at 13 years of age. He was in the wholesale clothing trade from 1854 to 1856, and then in the lumber trade until 1858. For the next three years he was employed at an importing house. In 1861, he became a professional gymnast in New York.[43] Whilst employed by a circus company in 1867, he worked with Dudley Allen Sargent, later to become an eminent pioneer of physical education in the United States.[44] Goldie also spent some time in Canada before 1869. When Dr. James McCosh came over from Scotland in 1868 to become President of Presbyterian Princeton, he soon advocated a gymnasium for the students. Through

---

Sawyer, p. 775, states that the program consisted of "field and track events of all kinds, with the exception of walking." Walter Kershaw, "Athletics In and Around New York," *Harper's Weekly*, June 21, 1890, p. 474, refers to 12 events of "the first out-door meeting 1868" but does not include the pole-vault.

41. Berthoff, p. 151.

42. *New York Times*, December 2, 1877, p. 2; November 6, 1878, p. 8.

43. Goshua L. Chamberlain, ed., *Universities and Their Sons* 2, (Boston: R. Herndon, 1898): p. 339.

44. Dudley Allen Sargent, *An Autobiography* (Philadelphia: Lea and Febiger, 1927), p. 67.

the generosity of Robert Bonner and Henry Marquand, each of whom donated $10,000 for the gymnasium, he was able to appoint George Goldie as its Director in 1869.[45]

At the time of his appointment, Goldie was a member of the New York Caledonian Club. He was also paid by the club to teach gymnastics in the hall for two or three nights a week.[46] The Annual Report of the Finance Committee of the Club for the year 1868 (Figure 5), included an item "Teacher $20,"[47] which alluded to Goldie's efforts in this respect. It also indicated the New York Caledonian Club's activities and efficient organization, and revealed a profit of nearly $2,000 from its Twelfth Annual Games. This far exceeded the sum of $151.61 realized from "the Eleventh Annual Ball," and was nearly four times the amount gained from "the concert given by Mr. Kennedy." The Games became the club's most important activity and greatest source of wealth. Other Caledonian Clubs in future years discovered the same financial fact.

Goldie was an outstanding athlete at these Games. At the Thirteenth, Fourteenth, and Fifteenth Annual Games of the New York Caledonian Club, he won many events.[48] At the unusual venue of Lion Park three years later in 1874, he also performed well. On a day when "the accom-

---

45. *The Princeton Alumni Weekly*, March 10, 1920, pp. 514–15; Thomas Jefferson Wertenbaker, *Princeton, 1746–1896* (Princeton, N.J.: Princeton University Press, 1946), pp. 324–25.

46. *Minutes of the Quarterly Meeting, New York Caledonian Club*, November 10, 1868; *Minutes of the Annual Meeting, New York Caledonian Club*, December 1, 1868; *Minutes of the Quarterly Meeting, New York Caledonian Club*, May 4, 1869; *Minutes of the Quarterly Meeting, New York Caledonian Club*, August 3, 1869.

47. *Annual Report of the Finance Committee of the New York Caledonian Club*, for the year 1868.

48. *Spirit of the Times*, September 10, 1870, pp. 54–55; *New York Times*, September 8, 1871, p. 5; *Minutes of Meeting, New York Caledonian Club*, September 8, 1871.

modation of the railroad not being sufficient, coaches, light wagons, and every conceivable kind of conveyance was pressed into service" to cater for a crowd of 20,000 persons, he was successful in four events. Winning the standing high leap and tossing the caber, he also came second in vaulting with the pole, and third in throwing the 56-lb. weight. There were 26 events altogether, in what were described as the most successful Games to date.[49] Henry Buermeyer, one of the founders of the New York Athletic Club, was again a judge at the Games.[50] He had also acted in that capacity for the Caledonians in 1871 and 1872.[51] George Goldie also won many prizes at the Boston and Philadelphia Games.[52]

As a professional gymnast appointed as Director of the Gymnasium at Princeton, Goldie's primary task was the teaching of gymnastics, and the daring activities of his pupils were often witnessed approvingly by Dr. James McCosh.[53] However, this active athlete also exerted himself in track and field activities and his campaigning was successful:

Mr. Goldie possessed the true spirit of a sportsman which we usually require only in an amateur. He was not satisfied with more than fulfilling his duty in the gymnasium, but began to interest himself in all the sports of the students. Then he began to suggest and show, until finally in the spring of '73 it was decided to hold an annual meeting for track athletics. This was called the Caledonian Games be-

49. *New York Times,* September 4, 1874, p. 8.
50. *Ibid.*
51. *Minutes of Meeting, New York Caledonian Club,* September 8, 1871; *Scottish-American Journal,* September 12, 1872.
52. *Boston Daily Globe,* August 29, 1873, p. 8; *Amherst Student,* October 31, 1874, p. 140.
53. *The Princeton Alumni Weekly,* March 10, 1920, p. 515; Wertenbaker, pp. 324–25.

cause at the time Mr. Goldie held the Caledonian Championship for all-round athletics.[54]

These first Princeton Caledonian Games were held on
June 21, 1873. All the events, except one, had been
featured in previous Caledonian Games in the United
States. The events were: standing long jump, running
long jump, putting the ball (16 lbs.), 125 yards run, running hop, skip, and jump, standing high leap, running high
leap, half-mile run, throwing the hammer, hitch and kick,
hurdles race, vaulting with pole, sack race, and throwing
the baseball.[55] The latter was not a usual Caledonian
event. The thoroughly Scottish activities such as the
broadsword dance, highland fling, and tossing the caber
were omitted, but otherwise any Caledonian competitor
would have felt at home at the Princeton Caledonian
Games.

Goldie demonstrated his own athletic ability two months
later at the Boston Caledonian Club's Twentieth Annual
Games. Winning the standing broad jump, vaulting with
the long pole, and the standing high leap, he also placed
in seven other events, to win at least $33 in what was one
of his best all-around performances. Due credit was accorded to "George Goldie, who figures so conspicuously
in the contests," and about 8,000 spectators witnessed his
feats.[56]

After their successful beginning, some slight changes
were made to the Princeton Games the following year. On
June 20, 1874, the 125-yard run became the 100-yard race;
the sack race was replaced by another Caledonian favorite,

54. Frank Presbrey, *Athletics at Princeton: A History* (New York
City: Frank Presbrey Co., 1901), p. 29.
55. *Scottish-American Journal,* June 26, 1873, p. 4.
56. *Boston Daily Globe,* August 29, 1873, p. 8.

the three-legged race; and a one-fourth-of-a-mile (440 yards) race was added. Gold medals of the value of $10 and $8 were awarded to successful competitors.[57]

Goldie remained at Princeton until 1885, when he became the first Director of Athletics at the New York Athletic Club. He acquired an excellent reputation and the success of the Club was largely attributed to his efforts.[58] He remained interested in his Caledonian Club's Games, acting as Referee in 1887.[59] Also in this year, a book was published containing an article by Goldie entitled "Gymnastics," which gave an insight into his views on the subject and into his job with the New York Athletic Club.[60] Princeton reclaimed his services in 1893, again as Director of the Gymnasium, until his retirement at age 70. During his second term there he became a charter member of the Society of Directors of Physical Education founded in 1897.[61] His name has been mentioned as one of the promoters, in 1899, of what may have been the first intercollegiate gymnastics meet in the United States.[62] When he died in his home at 35 University Place, at the age of 78, among the many floral tributes sent for his funeral was a large wreath from the veterans of the New York Athletic Club. Goldie Field at Princeton was named in his honor.[63] The *New York Times* did not allow the occasion to pass unnoticed:

57. *New York Times*, June 21, 1874, p. 7; *Scottish-American Journal*, June 25, 1874, p. 5.
58. Kershaw, p. 490.
59. *New York Times*, September 2, 1887, p. 3.
60. Henry Hall, ed., *The Tribune Book of Open Air Sports* (New York: The Tribune Association, 1887), pp. 332–39.
61. *American Physical Education Review*, February 1923, p. 58.
62. Raymond J. Runkle, "A History of Intercollegiate Gymnastics" (D.Ed. dissertation, Teachers' College, Columbia University, 1957), pp. 106–7.
63. *The Princeton Alumni Weekly*, March 10, 1920, p. 515.

VETERAN TRAINER DEAD

George Goldie Earned Fame at
Princeton and the New York A. C.
(special to the New York Times)

PRINCETON, N.J., Feb. 24—George Goldie, all-round athlete and Princeton University's first physical director, is dead at his home here at the age of 78. Heart trouble was the cause of his death.

Mr. Goldie is widely known in athletic circles both as a great athlete himself and as a great trainer of athletes. When a young man he was without peer as an all-round performer, and throughout his long career he labored to lay a constantly firmer base for American athletics. Mr. Goldie at one time was the holder of two world's records, one in the standing broad jump and one in the standing high jump. He inaugurated the use of the pole in jumping for height, and in this way became the father of the pole vault.

Mr. Goldie came to Princeton in 1869 from Montreal, of which city he was a native. Until the year 1885 he remained here and put the athletics of the university on an organized basis. In that year he left to go to the New York Athletic Club as its first coach. In 1893 he came back and was more or less actively associated with the university's athletic affairs until 1911, when he definitely retired.[64]

This tribute was in addition to his Obituary Note, which appeared on the previous page and stated further that "from 1869 to 1885 he held the three-year and five-year all-round athletic championships of the United States."[65]

Goldie had spent some years in Montreal, Canada. The Scotsmen there were not idle in fostering their cultural habits at this time, and similar Scottish associations

64. *New York Times*, February 25, 1920, p. 12.
65. *Ibid.*, p. 11.

matched and sometimes preceded their American counterparts.[66] In 1857 "The Grand Annual Gathering of the Caledonian Society came off with great success" in Guilbault's Gardens, Montreal. The events were: throwing the heavy hammer (21 lbs.), throwing the light hammer (14 lbs.), vaulting, short race, tossing the caber, running high leap, standing high leap, putting the heavy stone, putting the light stone, running long leap, standing leap, standing hop and leap, sack race, and barrow race.[67] Canadian audiences were also enthusiastic. At the Fourteenth Annual Games at Montreal in 1869, "ticket sellers were driven to despair by the demand for tickets"; and in 1870, at Toronto's Caledonian Gathering, "crowds of strangers poured into the city from the earliest hour by steamboats, rails and vehicles of all descriptions until, with local citizens, the grounds around Crystal Palace were packed with at least 12,000 persons awaiting the Games."[68]

In 1867, the Caledonian Clubs of both Canada and the United States held their first International Games at Jones' Woods, New York (Figure 6).[69] Three years later delegates from clubs of both countries attended a convention at which they discussed the advisability of the standardization of implement specifications and measurement procedures. An attempt was also made to standardize the rules governing the events of the Caledonian Games. In conclusion, they federated as the North American Cale-

---

66. Gordon Donaldson, *The Scots Overseas* (London: Robert Hale, 1966), p. 151.
67. Stewart Alexander Davidson, "A History of Sports and Games in Eastern Canada Prior to World War 1" (D.Ed. dissertation, Columbia University, 1951), Appendix E, p. 141; Henry Roxborough, *One Hundred Not Out: The Story of Nineteenth Century Canadian Sport* (Toronto: The Ryerson Press, 1966), p. 109.
68. Roxborough, p. 110.
69. Berthoff, p. 168; Dulles, pp. 202–3 (illustration).

donian Association.[70] The major concern of all Caledonian Clubs was the promotion of athletic games, and this was the first international organization of their sport. Its birth was further evidence of the tremendous popularity of the Caledonian Games in both countries, and the financial benefits of consistent public patronage.[71]

At the Sixth Annual Convention of the Association, it was felt that the "International Highland Games" held in conjunction with the conventions were a great success. Satisfaction was also expressed at the $23,000 cash balance of the New York Club, which also had the largest membership.[72] The Association demonstrated a priority concern later, when the proposition to amend the bylaws so that "all competitors at annual games must be members of Caledonian Clubs or Societies, and no honorary member shall have the right to compete in the Games of any Club" was defeated after a long discussion.[73] Despite the qualms of some of its members, the highest Caledonian authority of all kept the Caledonian Games open to all. At least two competitors had reason to feel grateful three years later, when a one-mile race of 20 starters included "two muscular Arizona Indians, Johse and Antonio," and "there was no doubt about their being real Indians."[74]

But although the Caledonian Games were open to all, amateur track and field athletics began with the founding of the New York Athletic Club in 1868, and within a few years many similar clubs appeared in the major cities of the United States.[75] Their members were not expected to

---

70. Berthoff, p. 168; Korsgaard, pp. 27–28.
71. Berthoff, p. 151.
72. *Spirit of the Times*, August 7, 1875, p. 673.
73. *New York Times*, August 17, 1877, p. 5.
74. *Ibid.*, September 3, 1880, p. 3.
75. Korsgaard, pp. 32–33.

compete for cash prizes. In 1874, when Yale University announced its intention to award cash prizes at its Annual Games, the *Spirit of the Times* devoted an editorial to this proposition, expressing the hope that a misunderstanding was evident. It warned that the amateur standing of the participants might be in danger, and called attention to the Scottish Inter-University Games of 1873, when a University of Aberdeen student was disqualified from running in an amateur meet because he had previously competed against Dinnie, Fleming, and other Caledonian athletes.[76] A few days later an official spokesman for Yale explained that the text should have read "Prizes of the following value. . . ."[77] A few months later:

> Some of the younger members of the Caledonian Society of New York, realizing that the cash prizes that were awarded at the games would jeopardize their amateur standing, broke off from the parent club and formed the Scottish-American Club. This club did not adhere to the mother's club requirement that members had to be of Scotch birth or descent. The Scottish-American Club soon became one of the prominent athletic clubs of the East.[78]

The latter statement was reinforced by another testimonial: "The crack Scottish-American A.C. of New York was, athletically speaking, a very fine organization."[79] It held successful meetings and enjoyed good relationships with other athletic clubs, particularly the New York Athletic Club.[80] On Thanksgiving Day, 1879, the 752

76. *Spirit of the Times,* December 5, 1874, p. 403.
77. Korsgaard, p. 37.
78. *Ibid.,* p. 28.
79. Janssen, p. 54.
80. *New York Times,* December 2, 1877, p. 2; November 6, 1878, p. 8; November 29, 1878, p. 8; Sawyer, p. 775; Janssen, p. 54.

entries at the Scottish-American Athletic Club's meeting was exceeded only by those of another famous club, the Manhattan Athletic Club.[81] This offspring of the richest and largest Caledonian Club in the country more than held its own against other clubs which had also adopted the sports of its forefathers.

At the time of Goldie's athletic achievements in the United States, the champion athlete of his native Scotland was undoubtedly Donald Dinnie. The latter's exploits at the Scottish Highland Games earned him worldwide acclaim, as did his prodigious feats of strength, often arranged as exhibitions at the Games. He was "the best all-round athlete Scotland has ever produced."[82]

At the quarterly meeting of the New York Caledonian Club held on February 2, 1869,

> Chieftain G. Mitchell offered the following suggestion: That the Club pay the passage of Donald Dinnie, the great Scottish athlete to attend and compete at our annual Games.[83]

The Finance Committee's Report for 1870 records an item of $130, for "Donald Dinnie's Passage Tickets."[84] He did not actually compete in the New York Club's Games until 1871, and again in 1872.[85] Nor was he alone on his American tours: "The champions of Scotland, itself, those braw lads Donald Dinnie (Figure 7) and James Fleming

81. Sawyer, p. 775.
82. David Webster, *Scottish Highland Games* (Glasgow and London: Collins, 1959), p. 94.
83. *Minutes of the Quarterly Meeting, New York Caledonian Club,* February 2, 1869.
84. *Report of the Finance Committee, New York Caledonian Club,* for the year 1870.
85. *Scottish-American Journal,* September 12, 1872; *Spirit of the Times,* September 10, 1870, pp. 54–55; *New York Times,* September 8, 1871, p. 5; September 3, 1880, p. 3.

(Figure 8), came over in the 1870s for a triumphant and profitable circuit of the Scottish-American Games."[86] These two paved the way for others to follow, and Dinnie himself returned in later years.[87]

At the New York Caledonian Club's Games in 1872, Dinnie also acted as judge for some of the competitions, along with Henry E. Buermeyer of the New York Athletic Club.[88] Before the year was out, the Caledonians also held a "Sociable and Games" at the Harlem Grounds of the New York Athletic Club.[89] Again, a few years later William B. Curtis, another founder of the latter club, was directing the Twenty-third Annual Games of the Caledonian Club with George Goldie.[90] Thus, the amateur and professional relationship in New York continued.

Donald Dinnie returned to the United States in 1877, and promoters offered him large sums to appear at their Games, with the result that he accumulated large amounts in a short time. In fact, he was able to earn over $700 in a day.[91] Five years later an advertisement for the Twelfth Annual Games of the Hudson County Caledonian Club, New Jersey, proudly announced that "Donald Dinnie will positively appear."[92] Many athletes wished that he would not. A few weeks earlier, Canadian athletes had sent a letter of protest concerning the impending visit of Dinnie and two other Scottish athletes, G. Davidson and W. Cummings, to Games in Canada. With such champions coming to carry off the larger prize monies, they lamented

86. Berthoff, p. 151.
87. Donaldson, p. 126; Webster, pp. 97–98; *New York Times,* September 2, 1881, p. 8; September 3, 1886, p. 2.
88. *Scottish-American Journal,* September 12, 1872.
89. *Ibid.,* December 5, 1872, p. 5.
90. *New York Times,* September 5, 1879, p. 8.
91. Webster, p. 98.
92. *Scottish-American Journal,* June 29, 1882, p. 5.

that "other athletes will find it impossible to make it remunerative to attend the Games."[93] But within a few weeks one athlete found it profitable to do so, despite Dinnie's presence:

THE CHAMPION OF SCOTLAND DEFEATED

A large crowd of spectators were present at Yonkers yesterday to witness the annual athletic games held under the auspices of the Yonkers Caledonian Society. The principal contest of the day was between Donald Dinnie of Scotland, the champion of the world, and Duncan C. Ross of Louisville, Kentucky. Much to the surprise of nearly all present young Ross defeated the champion in the two principal contests of the day, as follows:—Putting the heavy stone—Ross, 44'9½"; Dinnie, 43'7½". Throwing the heavy hammer—Ross, 109'10½"; Dinnie, 101'7". When the referee announced his decision Ross received a perfect ovation, and was carried off the grounds by his friends.[94]

This same "young Ross" had competed successfully at the Boston Games, and later, in 1888, won a $100 prize in the sword contest there.[95] The American tours made by Dinnie and other visiting athletes from Scotland greatly added to the appeal and success of the Caledonian Games. The odd setback apart, the visitors usually enjoyed great hospitality, and financial reward as well.

It was customary at the Annual Games of the larger clubs to receive delegations of chieftains, judges, competitors, and spectators from other Caledonian Clubs. For

---

93. *Ibid.*, May 18, 1882, p. 5.
94. *New York Times*, July 4, 1882, p. 8. Dinnie was only five days short of his 45th birthday at the time.
95. *Boston Daily Globe*, August 29, 1879, p. 4; August 27, 1880, p. 4; August 31, 1888, p. 8.

PUTTING THE HEAVY STONE.

THROWING THE HEAVY HAMMER.

THE HIGHLAND FLING.

SCOTTISH GAMES.

SOME months since the New York Caledonian Club offered a series of prizes to Scotchmen most excelling in the peculiar sports of the Scotch people; and the result was the assemblage at Jones's Wood, New York City, on July 1, of a large number of contestants and visitors from all parts of the country. The Scottish games have become an institution among us, and many others besides our Scotch residents assemble yearly to witness them. On this occasion at least 20,000 people were present, and the scene was a most enlivening one. Our engravings illustrate the most interesting of the various games and sports indulged in.

Putting the heavy stone and throwing the heavy hammer are feats very similar in appearance, both requiring very different qualities. The first demands brute strength. A stone weighing 24 pounds is thrown from the shoulder; the person throwing it farthest receiving a gold medal, the second receiving $20, and the third receiving $10. The winner on this occasion threw the weight a distance of 31 feet 4 inches. Throwing the heavy hammer requires more skill than strength. The performer in this game stands sideways and swings a large sledge-hammer weighing 22 pounds backward and forward until it gains sufficient impetus, when his utmost exertions are brought to impel its flight to the goal. The Highland

fling is indulged in by a great number, who displayed unusual grace and agility and endurance, and were highly applauded by the audience.

In the wheel-barrow race the contestants were crowned with large white mitres fastened down over their eyes, completely blindfolding them. The racers were started, after each had made a circle with his barrow at the starting-point, to reach the

club banner, which was placed at the other end of the arena. Only four or five came near the goal, while the others shot off into the crowd at different points or ran into and tumbled over each other.

The sack race was an amusing feature of the day's sports. Eight men, all muffled up to the neck in huge canvas bags, started at a signal from the judges, and hopped, stumbled, kicked, fell down, got up again, and finally reached the goal at the other end of the field from whence they had started with as much dignity as the circumstances would admit, amidst a general uproar and tumult of laughter from the ten thousand spectators surrounding the ring.

Besides the illustrations of these features of the games we give a group of the Resident Chiefs of the Caledonian Club, under whose auspices the contests were held; and a *fac-simile* of the medal distributed to the winners of the first prizes.

Various other games besides those which we have illustrated were played by the club and its visitors from abroad. Running jumps of 19 feet 3 inches, running high leaps of 5 feet 8 inches, and standing high leaps of 4 feet 7 inches were made; one of the contestants—a sort of human kangaroo, from Canada—with the aid of a pole, actually leaped 9 feet and 3 inches from the ground. A New York policeman grasped a small sapling tree, 15 feet long, and weighing 230 pounds, at one end, and threw it in

such a manner that it turned in the air and struck on the other end. A tambourine was suspended under cross-bars, and the contestants, taking a short run, leaped and kicked at it: the task was to kick the tambourine and alight on the same foot. One of the parties succeeded in doing this when the tambourine was elevated to a height of 9 feet 6 inches.

RESIDENT CHIEFS.

SCOTTISH GAMES AT JONES'S WOOD.

WHEEL-BARROW RACE.

SACK RACE.

FIGURE 1. Scottish Games.
(from *Harper's Weekly*, July 10, 1867)

FIGURE 2. Tossing the caber.
(from *Frank Leslie's Illustrated Newspaper*,
September 18, 1869)

FIGURE 3.   The Caledonian Club at Randall's Island.
(from *Harper's Weekly*, November 2, 1867)

FIGURE 4. Throwing the hammer.

Annual Report of the Finance Committee

OF THE

NEW YORK CALEDONIAN CLUB,

For the Year 1868.

Disbursements.

Appropriation to Property Committee of 1867,	
to ballance account, $	79,99
" to Library Committee of 1867,	19,70
Appropriations to " " 1868,	260,00
do to Property " " 1868,	300,00
Total Expenses of 11th Annual Ball,	573,39
Paid to Duke & More, for extending Club House,	2,575.82
Chandeliers, Gas Fixtures and Globes,	242,90
Extra Gas Fitting,	18,87
Opening Entertainment, Club House,	200.00
Expenses of First Kennedy Concert,	340.00
Paid by Treasurer to Mr. Kennedy's 2d Concert,	272.00
Gold Medal and Badge, presented to Mr. Kennedy,	60.00
Total Expenses 11th Annual Pic-Nic,	751,75
Rent of Club House, (21 months.)	700,00
Cost of Goods imported from Scotland,	506,17
Duty, Freight and Cartage on Imported Goods,	141.28
Salary of Recording Secretary, (1 year,)	100,00
" " Corresp'g " "	50,00
Total Amount of Charitable Donations,	241,00
Gas for Club House,	104,27
Printing, Postage, Envelopes, &c., for Special, Funeral and Monthly Notices,	304.15
Fitting up Gymnasium, $210. Teacher, $20.	230,00
Receipt Books, $18. Trustees' & Treas's' Book $2,	20.00
Stationery for Sec. $4. Repairing Seal Press $2.	6,00
Overpaid Dues refunded, $3. Initi'n fee returned, $5.	8,00
Total Expenses 12th Annual Games,	2,101,67
Piper to Kennedy Concert,	8.00
For legal services, suit against Meyers & Co.	35.50
Cash paid for one $1,000 U. S. 5-20 Bond,	1,130,00
Prizes for Curling Game,	50,00
TOTAL DISBURSEMENTS,	$11,430,46

Receipts.

Cash Balance, December, 1867,	$1,522,75
Total Receipts from Initiation Fees,	405,00
" " " Quarterly Dues,	606,04
Eleventh Annual Ball, to date,	724,00
First "Kennedy Concert,"	894,00
Second " "	275,00
Eleventh Annual Pic-Nic,	669,00
Receipts from sale of Imported Goods,	804.41
" " " two $1,000 U. S. 5-20 bonds,	2,126,25
Eleventh Annual Games Tickets,	23.00
Total Receipts Twelfth Annual Games,	4,078.40
Club Badges, $22.50 One Key, 25c.	22.75
Ballance returned by Sick and Visiting Committee,	15,00
Re-instatement Fees,	5,00
Interest on U. S. Bonds,	242,30
Certificates of Membership,	2,00
Over cash received by Secretary,	27
	$12,415,17
Deducting the Disbursements,	11,430,46
Leaves a Cash Balance, Dec. 15th, 1868,	$984,71

There are also in the Treasurer's hands }
Three $1,000 U. S. 5-20 Bonds }

It will be seen from the foregoing statement, that the Club has re-alized from the Eleventh Annual Ball, the sum of $151.61, and from the Concert given by Mr. Kennedy, $554,00,

From the Tickets sold to Members for Mr. Kennedy's Second Concert, there has been received $3.00 more than the sum paid to Mr. K. by the Treasurer.

At the date of this report, the Eleventh Annual Pic-Nic Receipts are short of the Expenses, $82,75,

From the Twelfth Annual Games, the Club has re-alized the handsome amount of $1976.73.

The Receipts from Initiation Fees, show that the Club has added 81 new members to its roll during the year.

The Total Expenses attending the enlargement of the Club House, were $2837,47.

Your Committee has examined the accounts of the Library and Property Committees, and find them to be correct. The Library Committee has received appropriations to the amount of $260.00, and have expended $227.29. The Property Committee has received $300.00, and has expended $290.51.

The Total Expenditures for the support of the Club House, including one year's Rent and Gas, and the necessary Repairs and Supplies, amount to about $650.00.

In concluding this Report, your Committee desire to congratulate the Club on its prosperous condition, and to express the hope, that the same prosperity and harmony may mark its careeer throughout the present year.

They would also bear testimony to the correctness of the accounts of the Treasurer and Secretary, and to the scrupulous honesty of all who have had the disbursing of the Club's funds.

All of which is respectfully submitted,

On Motion the report was received and ordered to be printed.

Clansman JOHN McLELLAN, Chairman. }
Past Chief WILLIAM MANSON, } Finance Committee
Past Chief'n JOHN WATT, }

FIGURE 5. Annual Report of the Finance Committee of the New York Caledonian Club, for the year 1868.

FIGURE 6. The Great International Caledonian Games, held at Jones Wood, New York City, July 1, 1867. (Courtesy Museum of the City of New York)

FIGURE 7. Donald Dinnie at 61 years of age.

FIGURE 8. James Fleming.

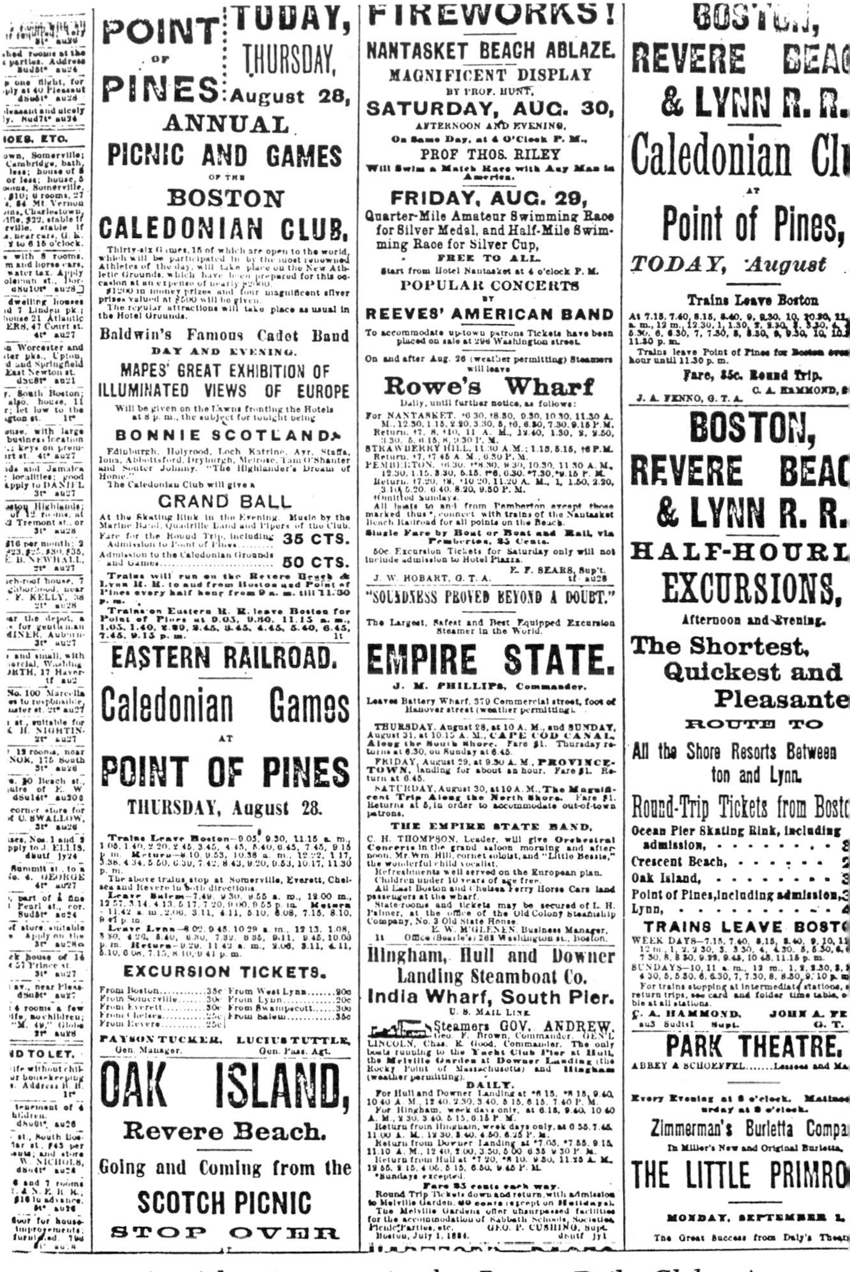

POINT OF PINES: TODAY, THURSDAY, August 28,

ANNUAL

PICNIC AND GAMES

OF THE

BOSTON

CALEDONIAN CLUB.

Thirty-six Games, 15 of which are open to the world, which will be participated in by the most renowned Athletes of the day, will take place on the New Athletic Grounds, which have been prepared for this occasion at an expense of nearly $2000.

$1200 in money prizes and four magnificent silver prizes valued at $500 will be given.

The regular attractions will take place as usual in the Hotel Grounds.

Baldwin's Famous Cadet Band

DAY AND EVENING.

MAPES' GREAT EXHIBITION OF ILLUMINATED VIEWS OF EUROPE

Will be given on the Lawns fronting the Hotels at 8 p. m., the subject for tonight being

BONNIE SCOTLAND

Edinburgh, Holyrood, Loch Katrine, Ayr, Staffa, Iona, Abbottsford, Dryburgh, Melrose, Tam O'Shanter and Souter Johnny, "The Highlander's Dream of Home."

The Caledonian Club will give a

GRAND BALL

At the Skating Rink in the Evening. Music by the Marine Band, Quadrille Band and Pipers of the Club.

Fare for the Round Trip, including Admission to Point of Pines ..... 35 CTS.

Admission to the Caledonian Grounds and Games ..... 50 CTS.

Trains will run on the Revere Beach & Lynn R. R. to and from Boston and Point of Pines every half hour from 9 a. m. till 11.30 p. m.

Trains on Eastern R. R. leave Boston for Point of Pines at 9.05, 9.30, 11.15 a. m., 1.05, 1.40, 2.20, 2.45, 3.45, 4.45, 5.40, 6.45, 7.45, 9.15 p. m.

EASTERN RAILROAD.

Caledonian Games

AT

POINT OF PINES

THURSDAY, August 28.

EXCURSION TICKETS.

PAYSON TUCKER, Gen. Manager. LUCIUS TUTTLE, Gen. Pass. Agt.

OAK ISLAND,

Revere Beach.

Going and Coming from the

SCOTCH PICNIC

STOP OVER

FIREWORKS!

NANTASKET BEACH ABLAZE.

MAGNIFICENT DISPLAY

BY PROF. HUNT,

SATURDAY, AUG. 30,

AFTERNOON AND EVENING.

On Same Day, at 4 O'Clock P. M.,

PROF THOS. RILEY

Will Swim a Match Race with Any Man in America.

FRIDAY, AUG. 29,

Quarter-Mile Amateur Swimming Race for Silver Medal, and Half-Mile Swimming Race for Silver Cup,

FREE TO ALL.

Start from Hotel Nantasket at 4 o'clock P. M.

POPULAR CONCERTS BY REEVES' AMERICAN BAND

To accommodate up-town patrons Tickets have been placed on sale at 296 Washington street.

On and after Aug. 26 (weather permitting) Steamers will leave

Rowe's Wharf

Daily, until further notice, as follows:

J. W. HOBART, G. T. A. E. F. SEARS, Sup't.

"SOUNDNESS PROVED BEYOND A DOUBT."

The Largest, Safest and Best Equipped Excursion Steamer in the World.

EMPIRE STATE.

J. M. PHILLIPS, Commander.

THE EMPIRE STATE BAND.

E. W. M'GLENEN, Business Manager.

Hingham, Hull and Downer Landing Steamboat Co.

India Wharf, South Pier.

U. S. MAIL LINE.

Steamers GOV. ANDREW, LINCOLN

DAILY.

Fare 25 cents each way.

GEO. P. CUSHING, Supt.

BOSTON, REVERE BEACH & LYNN R. R.

Caledonian Club

AT

Point of Pines,

TODAY, August

Trains Leave Boston

Fare, 25c. Round Trip.

J. A. FENNO, G. T. A. C. A. HAMMOND

BOSTON, REVERE BEACH & LYNN R. R.

HALF-HOURLY EXCURSIONS,

Afternoon and Evening.

The Shortest, Quickest and Pleasantest

ROUTE TO

All the Shore Resorts Between Boston and Lynn.

Round-Trip Tickets from Boston

Ocean Pier Skating Rink, including admission,

Crescent Beach,

Oak Island,

Point of Pines, including admission,

Lynn,

TRAINS LEAVE BOSTON

PARK THEATRE.

ABBEY & SCHOEFFEL .... Lessees and Ma

Every Evening at 8 o'clock. Matinee Saturday at 2 o'clock.

Zimmerman's Burletta Company

In Miller's New and Original Burletta,

THE LITTLE PRIMROSE

MONDAY, SEPTEMBER 1.

The Great Success from Daly's Theatre

FIGURE 9. Advertisements in the *Boston Daily Globe*, August 30, 1888.

example, the New York Caledonian Club expressed the hope after its Games in 1872, that

> while Caledonians might carry away a few hints as to the management of Scottish games which they may hereafter turn to practical account, the whole vast body of visitors might carry to their distant houses a pleasant remembrance of New York, and of the annual fete of its Caledonian club.[96]

There were delegations from Caledonian Clubs at Montreal, Ottawa, Chicago, Philadelphia, Newark, Bridgeport, Scranton, Cooperstown, Pittston, Portland, Hartford, and districts of New York. Various St. Andrew's Societies were represented as well. Apart from mayors and other civic dignitaries, professors, and reverends who attended Scottish Games regularly, there were often other distinguished guests. These New York Games of 1872 were witnessed by Sir John Peter Grant, the Governor of Jamaica. The famous apostle of the Muscular Christianity Movement, Thomas Wentworth Higginson, also visited the Games of the Providence Caledonian Club, held to celebrate the centenary of Sir Walter Scott's birth.[97] The British Consul attended the New York Games of 1879, and the Marquis of Queensberry "expressed himself as very much pleased with the sports" at Boston six years later.[98]

Although begun as patriotic field days for Scotsmen, American visitors were always welcome at the Caledonian Games, initially as spectators but soon as competitors:

> Americans as well as Scots soon flocked by the thousands

96. *Scottish-American Journal*, September 12, 1872.
97. Thomas Wentworth Higginson, "A Day of Scottish Games," *Scribner's*, January 1872, pp. 329–36.
98. *New York Times*, September 5, 1879, p. 8; *Boston Daily Globe*, August 28, 1885, p. 5.

to Caledonian Games in cities the country over. If the Scots frowned on these motley crowds, they welcomed the flood of silver at the gates and soon threw the competitions open to all athletes, be they Scots, Americans, Irish, Germans, or Negroes. Down to the 1870's, however, practiced Scotsmen won most of the prizes.[99]

A number of robust, but awkward hammer-throwers at the Philadelphia Games of 1866 could not match these "practiced Scotsmen," and "Scotland beat the field."[100] The games that Higginson witnessed at Providence four years later were also "open to all comers," and his most lavish praise was reserved for the Scottish victor in the hammer-throwing event.[101] One of the greatest American track and field athletes of the nineteenth century later maintained that scientific hammer-throwing undoubtedly originated in Scotland, as did the pole-vault and shot-put.[102] In these events particularly, the more experienced Scottish athletes were able to hold their own for a number of years, until the amateur athletic clubs became established and stiffer competition resulted. For example, in 1877, members of the New York Caledonian Club successfully competed in the hammer, shot, and other events at the New York Athletic Club's games.[103]

In the earlier years, only one or two events at the Caledonian Games would be open to all, but the number gradually increased as support grew. Organizers of the Boston

---

99. Berthoff, p. 151.
100. *Scottish-American Journal,* September 1, 1866. See also Peter Ross, *The Scot in America* (New York: The Raeburn Book Company, 1896), p. 427.
101. Higginson, pp. 331–32.
102. Malcolm W. Ford, "Hammer-Throwing" *Outing,* September, 1892, p. 450; "Pole-vaulting" *Outing,* April, 1892, p. 42; "Shot-Putting" *Outing,* July 1892, p. 287.
103. *New York Times,* May 13, 1877, p. 2.

Games evolved a system where the events in the morning were for the Caledonian Club members only, and those in the afternoon were "open to the world."[104] Since 1868, some Caledonian athletes had participated in athletic clubs' meetings. Also,

> an athletic club member might run in his club's closed games one week, and run in a matched race or row in a sculling race for $500 a side the next week. . . . Betting had nothing to do with one's amateur status; even after a concept of amateurism had been promulgated by the New York Athletic Club in 1872. Despite the fact that this club awarded only medals, the contestants and their backers continued to bet on the outcome of an event so that in many instances the stakes were considerably higher than the medal offered.[105]

The arrival of the athletic clubs did not immediately guarantee amateurism, or deny professionalism. Defining an amateur was a tortuous task which took several years.[106] In the meantime, the Caledonians also included events in their Games which were "open only to members of amateur organizations," and members of the New York Athletic Club, West Side Athletic Club, Manhattan Athletic Club, Pastime Athletic Club, and others entered for them.[107]

Some of the visitors came to earn money as other than a professional athlete. The immense crowds were a delight to entrepreneurs. At New York, "besides the drill there were countless other attractions" which included

---

104. *Boston Daily Globe,* August 29, 1884, p. 4.
105. Korsgaard, p. 35.
106. *Ibid.,* pp. 34–47.
107. *New York Times,* September 2, 1881, p. 8; September 3, 1886, p. 2.

"swees," "merry-go-rounds," "half-a-dozen Irish fiddlers" and other amusements.[108] The peddlers, hucksters, and impromptu restaurants connected with the Boston Games were severely taxed to accommodate the thousands of pleasure seekers.[109] With professional athletes in the ring before such large crowds, gambling was not unknown. This was true of other sports in the United States at the time. At the New York Caledonian Club's Games in 1859, "the greatest interest was manifested by the spectators; but no betting was allowed or heard of about the grounds."[110] But for a five-mile race in 1881, "much money was staked on the result by the enthusiastic crowd" attending the Quarter Centennial Festival of the Club.[111]

The Caledonians were meticulous in their organization for the Games. Despite the huge crowds, and the revelry which usually followed the Games, order was generally maintained. The newspapers for the most part published glowing accounts of their efforts, praising the behavior of crowds of 20,000 or more. Because "the Members of the Caledonian Club exerted themselves to the utmost to preserve order," at most Games, and police were in attendance as well, peace usually prevailed.[112] One Scottish Society which also held its Games was the Clan-Na-Gael Society. This kept turbulent characters under control by an efficient force "composed of stalwart members of the Society."[113] However, fist fights and disorder sometimes

108. *Scottish-American Journal,* September 9, 1885, p. 8; *New York Times,* September 4, 1874, p. 8.
109. *Boston Daily Globe,* August 29, 1873, p. 8; August 31, 1883, p. 4.
110. Wilkes' *Spirit of the Times,* September 24, 1859.
111. *New York Times,* September 2, 1881, p. 8.
112. *Ibid.,* September 4, 1874, p. 8.
113. *Ibid.,* July 28, 1880, p. 3.

ensued at Scottish Games.[114] On one rare occasion, a young man trying to preserve order was stabbed to death.[115] But on the whole, the organizers managed their responsibilities very well, and the vast majority of the Annual Games' meetings were orderly and successful. The members of the Caledonian Clubs, especially, were expected to conduct themselves in an exemplary manner.[116]

The Caledonians soon began to consistently advertise their Games, and this campaign helped to attract large crowds. As early as 1868, the New York Caledonian Club spent nearly $100 on advertising its Twelfth Annual Games in the *Sunday Mercury, Scottish-American Journal, Sunday Dispatch, Sunday Times and Messenger, Sunday News, Sunday New York Courier,* and *Staatz Zeitung.*[117] *Harper's Weekly* had been used to give notice of the International Games in the previous year.[118] Not all the columns were used to attract the American public prior to the event, however, as the following example indicates:

SCOTSMEN!

Do not forget that all the famous athletes are now stopping at the Waverley House, Revere Beach.

DANCING TONIGHT

Duncan C. Ross, Manager.[119]

Their fellow-countrymen and others were kept well in-

114. *Ibid.,* July 5, 1878, p. 2; September 2, 1887, p. 3.
115. *Ibid.,* September 8, 1871, p. 5.
116. *The Minutes of the Meetings of the New York Caledonian Club,* 1867–1876, gives an insight into the high standards of behavior expected, and the disciplinary action taken against offenders.
117. *Report of Committee on Twelfth Annual Games, New York Caledonian Club,* 1868.
118. *Harper's Weekly,* June 29, 1867, p. 415.
119. *Boston Daily Globe,* August 30, 1888, p. 7.

formed about forthcoming attractions by the industrious and prudent Scotsmen. Other people, too, advertised in connection with the popular Caledonian Games; railway proprietors, for example, ran frequent excursions to the Games, and advertised their rates and times of arrival and departure.[120] A "stop over" was advertised on the way to the "Scotch Picnic" (Figure 9).[121]

Before the Civil War, a few American cities had Scottish Regiments. A New York Artillery Company, the Highland Guards, wore Cameron kilts and scarlet tunics, and participated in the strife as "the 79th Highland Regiment."[122] Afterwards they held yearly reunions and picnics. Like good Scots, even when "recently disbanded," the Old Guard celebrated the latter occasions with the Games, and the familiar events of putting the light stone, 100 yards, running long jump, throwing the light hammer, relief race (in pairs), hitch and kick, standing long jump, boys' race (under 14 yrs. of age; about 300 yards), one-mile walking race (open to the National Guard), hurdle race, hop, step, and jump, running high leap, tossing the caber, three-legged race, one-mile race (open to the National Guard), broadsword dance, highland fling, vaulting with the pole, and a "fat man's race, over two hundred pounds."[123] Not only did the 79th Highlanders perform on their home ground, but they regularly visited the Games at Boston, Philadelphia, Providence, and other

---

120. *Ibid.*, August 28, 1884, p. 3.
121. *Ibid.*
122. Berthoff, p. 179.
123. *Ibid.*; *New York Times*, July 29, 1876, p. 8; July 5, 1878, p. 2; July 30, 1879, p. 8; October 3, 1879, p. 3; Robert Ernst, *Immigrant Life in New York City* (New York: King's Crown Press, Columbia University, 1949), p. 129.

citics as well.[124] The "Scots Battalion" of Chicago held picnics and Games, also.[125]

Other soldiers were athletically inclined, too, and participated in the Scottish events and others. In 1878, "the greatest enthusiasm prevailed" over the tug-o-war competitions between squads representing several companies of the Seventh Regiment, at the New York Athletic Club's Games.[126] (Also on the program was an individual tug-o-war contest between W. B. Curtis, of the New York Athletic Club, and C. A. J. Queckberner, of the Scottish-American Athletic Club, which the former won). Twelve years later a track and field authority declared:

> The growth of athletics has been nowhere more clearly manifest than in our Militia requirements. The building of such immense armories as those of the Seventh in New York and the Thirteenth in Brooklyn has given the regimental athletes room enough to hold games indoors, and has greatly stimulated winter exercises of all sorts. Nearly all the Regiments now have athletic clubs, the most notable of which are those of the Seventh, the Twenty-second, the Twelfth, and the Thirteenth. The Seventh contains many members who belong also to the New York or Manhattan or other local clubs. An idea of the variety and excellence of its games may be had from a mere list of the events . . . in the meeting of Saturday, April 5th. Here is the program: 100 yds. run, 220 yds. run, half-mile walk, putting the 16 lb. shot, 440 yds. run, 220 yds. hurdle, running high jump, wheelbarrow race, half-mile roller-skating race, three-legged race and the two-mile bicycle race.[127]

---

124. *Boston Daily Globe*, August 29, 1874, p. 8; August 29, 1878, p. 2; *Scottish-American Journal*, September 9, 1885, p. 5.

125. *Scottish-American Journal*, September 15, 1881, p. 8.

126. *New York Times*, November 6, 1878, p. 8.

127. Kershaw, p. 473.

The sporting activities of the Caledonian Clubs and other Scottish Societies, the Scottish-American Athletic Club, the Scottish Regiments, and George Goldie at Princeton, in the two or three decades after the Civil War, made this the most influential and significant period of the Caledonian Games in the nineteenth century. Other colleges besides Princeton participated in similar pastimes, and the Caledonian Games "found their way into New England universities."[128] Out of their field days and rowing regattas came intercollegiate track and field.

---

128. Charles W. Hackensmith, *History of Physical Education* (New York: Harper and Row, 1966), p. 176.

5
Field Days, Regattas, and Intercollegiate Track and Field

The post-Civil War period was also characterized by an increase in student sporting activity, because of a number of factors. In the year that George Goldie was first appointed to Princeton, track and field first appeared at another college nearby. In fact, two other colleges participated in athletic field days before the Caledonian Games of Princeton began in 1873. In that year also was held the first intercollegiate track event in the United States, won by a Caledonian athlete. More footraces were featured in the next three years. These events were appendages to the intercollegiate rowing regattas and the promotion of a famous, sports-minded newspaper editor. The first field meeting of the Intercollegiate American Amateur Athletic Association was held in 1876, and won by Princeton. Track and field had joined the other intercollegiate sports in the United States. Its appearance was owing to the influence of the Caledonians, the idea of competition instilled by the regatta footraces, and the example of English undergraduates in their interuniversity sport.

American colleges and universities had no organized program of athletics in their earliest days, which were characterized by informal participation and spontaneity.

As student interest in competitive sports increased, athletic associations were formed which sponsored interclass games and field days. These associations were begun, controlled, and financed by the student. When interest multiplied further, some institutions competed against neighboring ones, and so originated intercollegiate athletics. The first intercollegiate athletic contest in the United States was a race between the boat clubs of Harvard and Yale Universities in 1852.[1]

The students in these institutions were the recipients of many unfavorable comments and descriptions by distinguished authors, prior to the rise in sport. "The incredible athletic phenomena of the 1870's are made more understandable by emphasizing the important contributions of certain writers during the period 1850–1860."[2] This literary campaign became known as the Muscular Christianity Movement, and the impact of one famous book associated with it, *Tom Brown's Schooldays*, was immense.[3]

Constant derisory comparisons with their British counterparts, which formed a relentless part of the campaign, stimulated American students to emulate or surpass them in physical prowess. Invective like "an apathetic-brained, a pale pasty-faced, narrow-chested, spindle-shanked, dwarfed race,"[4] and "black-coated, stiff-jointed, soft-

---

1. John Allen Krout, *Annals of American Sport* 15, *The Pageant of America Series*, 15 vols. (New York: United States Publishers Association, 1929): 80.
2. John A. Lucas, "A Prelude to the Rise of Sport: Ante-bellum America, 1850–1860," *Quest*, December 1968, pp. 50–57.
3. *Ibid.*, pp. 51–52; Guy Lewis, "The Muscular Christianity Movement," *Journal of Health, Physical Education and Recreation*, May 1966, pp. 27–28, 42.
4. "Why We Get Sick," *Harper's Magazine* 13 (October 1856): 646.

muscled, paste-complexioned . . ."[5] left its mark. Within twenty years this critical prelude had altered and the students were under different attack, as "the colleges turned to athletics with such abandon that the cartoonists soon revised their stereotype to that of a muscular paragon with no intelligence."[6]

The Harvard versus Oxford boat race over the Putney-Mortlake Course in London on August 27, 1869, attracted the attention of other American colleges to the sport, and interest in rowing increased.[7] Other Eastern schools besides Harvard and Yale were anxious to participate. At Goldie's arrival in 1869, "boating was an all-absorbing topic at Princeton."[8] Thomas Hughes, the English author, visited Cornell in 1870, and next year the Tom Hughes Boat Club was formed.[9] Amherst and Massachusetts Agricultural College also formed Boat Clubs in 1870, "and Trinity became active again."[10] An intercollegiate sports association was formed the following year, when Amherst, Bowdoin, Brown, and Harvard formed the Rowing Association of American Colleges.[11] The regattas of this Asso-

5. Oliver W. Holmes, "The Autocrat of the Breakfast Table," *Atlantic Monthly* (May 1858), p. 881.

6. Krout, p. 188.

7. Fred Eugene Leonard and George B. Affleck, *The History of Physical Education* (London: Henry Kimpton, 1947), p. 281; John A. Blanchard, ed., *The H Book of Harvard Athletics* (The Harvard Varsity Club, 1923), pp. 46–50.

8. Edwin M. Morris, *The Story of Princeton* (Boston: Little, Brown & Co., 1917), p. 247.

9. Robert J. Kane, *Forty Short Years* (Ithaca, N.Y.: Cornell University Press, 1939). The author has been Director of Athletics at Cornell since 1944. His monograph was provided by the Curator and Archivist of the John M. Olin Research Library at Cornell University.

10. Leonard and Affleck, p. 281.

11. *Ibid.*, p. 281; John Alfred Torney, "A History of Competitive Rowing in Colleges and Universities of the United States of America" (D.Ed. dissertation, Columbia University, 1958), pp. 158–59.

ciation greatly affected another future intercollegiate sport, track and field athletics, for which another "first" was recorded in 1869:

> To Columbia may be ascribed the credit of having been the first college to introduce track athletics in America. The great English Universities of Oxford and Cambridge had long ere this held annual meetings, which were very successful; but it was already late in 1868 when George Rives, a Columbia graduate, paid a visit to England and was so impressed with the great popularity of the games held there that he immediately wrote an enthusiastic letter, earnestly advocating the formation of an athletic association in this country. The result of his efforts was the formation of the Columbia College Athletic Association in 1869.[12]

His "visit" actually lasted four years, after which he graduated with a B.A. from Trinity College, Cambridge, in 1872, "where he distinguished himself as a scholar and athlete."[13] Foot-racing was known at Columbia and elsewhere before 1869, but the first field meeting at Columbia in June 1869 featured field events as well, at which no record was kept "of times, distances or heights."[14] The second meeting in the fall of the same year had the following events: 100 yards, 150 yards, hurdle race of 200 yards, a mile-walk, standing long jump, running long jump, high jump, and consolation races. In 1871, "a three-legged race was added with a steeplechase."[15]

---

12. *Blue and White* 2 (1891–92): 568–69; Leonard and Affleck, p. 282. Elsewhere it is claimed that Rives's plea was for the formation of an Athletic Association to promote rowing; see Torney, p. 169. His letter enthusiastically endorsed both rowing and track and field; see *The Cap and Gown,* April, 1869, p. 69.
13. *Columbia Alumni News,* September 28, 1917, p. 18.
14. *Blue and White* 2 (1891–92): 659.
15. *Ibid.*

Considering the direct description and recommendation from George Rives, the first program at an American college was not so similar as one might expect:

Columbia (1869–1871)	Oxford versus Cambridge (1869, 1870, and 1871)
1. 100 yards	100 yards
2. Long jump	Long jump
3. High jump	High jump
4. Hurdle race (200 yards)	Hurdle race (120 yards)
5. 150 yards	440 yards
6. 1 mile-walk	1 mile-run
7. Standing long jump	3 miles
8. Three-legged race (1871)	Weight (Putting the)
9. Steeplechase (1871)	Hammer (Throwing the)
10. Consolation races	————

Many events could have derived from other Athletics Clubs' Games in England, such as those held by the London Athletic Club or the Thames Rowing Club,[16] or from the Caledonian Games in the United States.[17]

The addition of the three-legged race by Columbia in 1871 was significant. This event had its origins (along with other "picnic events" like sack races, wheelbarrow races, etc.) in medieval Britain, or earlier. Such events were featured at fairs, wakes, and so on.[18] As late as 1826,

16. H. F. Wilkinson, *Modern Athletics* (London: Frederick Warne and Co., 1868), pp. 100–10.

17. *New York Times*, September 8, 1865, p. 2; September 4, 1868, p. 8; August 18, 1871, p. 6; September 8, 1871, p. 5.

18. Albert B. Wegener, *Track and Field Athletics* (New York: A. S. Barnes and Company, 1924), p. 146.

they formed part of a local wake at Norfolk.[19] As the nineteenth century progressed, however, "they doubtless grew rarer and rarer," although they also might "occasionally find a place in an athletic programme" in country meetings "where the spectators often like the introduction of the comic element."[20] The picnic events were dying out when Oxford and Cambridge commenced their track rivalry in 1864, and were never a part of their meetings.[21] A similar course of events occurred in the United States. The early Colonial fairs in several States included footraces and other athletic contests, as well as novelty events like climbing a greased pole, greased pig chases, sack races, and others.[22] Such happenings were not common in later nineteenth-century America. However, sack races, three-legged races, wheelbarrow races and other novelty events were a regular part of the Scottish Highland Games, and the Caledonian Games in the United States. This comic element introduced by Columbia in 1871 was the first of many such events to appear at similar institutions later.

At Yale, *The College Courant* of March 16, 1872, contained a report that "the officers of the ball and boat clubs have determined to give next term an exhibition of ath-

19. Montague Shearman, *Athletics and Football* (London: Longmans, Green and Company, 1889), p. 26.
20. *Ibid.*, p. 163.
21. Caspar W. Whitney, *A Sporting Pilgrimage* (New York: Harper and Brothers, 1894), pp. 220–31; Harold M. Abrahams and J. Bruce-Kerr, *Oxford versus Cambridge: a Record of Inter-University Contests from 1827 to 1930* (London: Faber and Faber, Ltd., 1931).
22. Charles M. Andrews, *Colonial Folkways* (New Haven: Yale University Press, 1919), pp. 120–29; Carl Bridenbaugh, *Cities in the Wilderness: The First Century of Urban Life in America, 1625–1742* (New York: The Ronald Press, 1938), pp. 119, 278; Edward Eggleston, "Social Life in the Colonies" *Century* (July 1885), pp. 378–407; Sydney George Fisher, *Men, Women and Manners in Colonial Times* 1 (Philadelphia: J. B. Lippincott, 1898): 71–73.

letic reports for the benefit of their respective organizations." Two months later it was stated:

> The first meeting of the Yale Athletic Association, a new organization under the control of the Ball and Boat clubs, was held at Hamilton Park last Saturday. The exercises were successful in every particular and much enthusiasm was aroused. There were enough entries in every contest to make it interesting and the day's sport was a financial success.[23]

The events on this occasion were: throwing the baseball, half-mile race, running high jump, running long jump, hurdle race (150 yards), three-legged race, 200-yards dash, standing high jump, standing long jump, walking race, hurdle race (200 yards), and a consolation race (200 yards). Elsewhere it was recorded that the first meeting at Yale was under the auspices of the Navy, Base and Football Clubs in the autumn of 1873 and 1874, which omitted the running long jump, three-legged race, 200 yards, standing high jump, and consolation race, but included a 100 yards dash, hop, step, and jump, and wrestling. Putting the shot appeared next, when "Yale in '75 formed an athletic association."[24] The Fourth Annual Scottish Games at New Haven also took place at Hamilton Park in 1874, although there was no evidence of Yale's participation.[25] But the events were strikingly similar.[26]

Yale was not represented at the first regatta of the Rowing Association of American Colleges in 1871, but it was one of the eight colleges which competed in 1872, along with other newcomers like Amherst, Bowdoin, Wesleyan, and Williams. These smaller colleges were encouraged

23. *The College Courant*, May 18, 1872.
24. Whitney, pp. 231–32.
25. *Scottish-American Journal*, June 25, 1874, p. 5.
26. *Ibid.*

by the victory of Massachusetts Agricultural College over Harvard and Brown a year earlier.[27] Their optimism was justified, when Amherst won the University race, and Wesleyan won the freshman race. Harvard came second, Yale was sixth, and intercollegiate rowing was attracting more participants.

In 1873, Goldie's campaign at Princeton resulted in the first track and field meeting there, named the "Caledonian Games" in his honor, held on June 21. These Games became the model for other colleges yet to embark upon their track and field activity. At this time three colleges only were participating in the sport: Columbia, Yale, and Princeton. At Yale, the Athletic Association responsible for the first meeting in 1872 was under the control of the Ball and Boat clubs.[28] Columbia's entry was owing to the suggestion of George Rives, and George Goldie definitely was the founder at Princeton.

Princeton and Yale already had gymnasiums before the emergence of track and field. Princeton's second gymnasium was built in 1869, when Goldie was appointed to take charge of it, and Yale's nine years earlier.[29] The possession of a gymnasium by a college at this time indicated a concern for health and regard for the value of physical activity, as did the appointment of a specialist instructor. The initial rise of track and field, in fact, took place largely in those institutions having this facility. In the period between 1859 and 1870, gymnasia were erected at Amherst, Dartmouth, Harvard, Pennsylvania, Princeton, Wesleyan, and Yale. Williams had adapted an existing

27. Torney, p. 161.
28. *The College Courant*, March 16, 1872; and May 18, 1872.
29. Leonard and Affleck, pp. 270–74; Edward Mussey Hartwell, *Physical Training in American Colleges and Universities* (Washington: Government Printing Office, 1886), p. 27, 40, 60.

building.[30] Besides the already-involved Princeton and Yale, the other six institutions all took up track and field within two years after 1873. Within ten years, when track and field had been established, these gymnasia were used for indoor "winter exhibitions" at several colleges, in which gymnastics and track and field were combined.[31]

But rowing, more than gymnastics, was significantly connected with intercollegiate track and field. Also in 1873 occurred the first form of intercollegiate track competition, at the regatta, and another individual promoter appeared on the scene, James Gordon Bennett, Jr. He had "made the *Herald* the foremost New York oracle for sportsmen in the late 1860's," and as an "athletic outdoor man" had "established numerous prizes for yachting and racing contestants."[32] As a "long distance pedestrian" himself, Bennett also "offered cups in the 70's to winners in college rowing races and track and field events."[33] The first for the latter was to the winner of a two-mile run, the sole track event at the 1873 regatta.

This first intercollegiate footrace in the United States was won by a Caledonian athlete from the Montreal Caledonian Club, named D. E. Bowie. In the previous year he had great success at the 16th annual celebration of the New York Caledonian Club, winning the one mile, the hop, step, and jump, the long race and short race, and coming second in the running long jump. The former was deemed a "special race," and his tactics gained approval:

30. Hartwell, p. 60.

31. Raymond J. Runkle, "A History of Intercollegiate Gymnastics" D. Ed. dissertation, Columbia University, 1957), pp. 97–98.

32. John Rickards Betts, "Sporting Journalism in Nineteenth-Century America," *American Quarterly*, No. 5 (Spring 1953), p. 52.

33. William Henry Nugent, "The Sports Section" *American Mercury*, March 1929, p. 336.

All the races were very meritorious, and Bowie the clever young Canadian Scot, sufficiently signalised himself to take his stand as a member of whom the Montreal club ought to be proud. We especially admired his cool way in the mile race of allowing his two leading opponents to race with each other for the lead, and then quietly passing them on the last lap, of running in an easy winner with any distance to spare.[34]

The prize money for this meeting in 1872 amounted to $1,500, of which sum $1,000 in cash was given to the athletes, and the remaining $500 "in goods consisting of parts of the Highland costume." The value of the prizes in the special race won by Bowie was $90.[35] His skill had not deserted him in the two-mile race at the regatta next year, where he represented McGill University.

There were five entries for the race: Bowie; Benton of Amherst; Lawrence of Dartmouth; Phillips and Dudley of Cornell; and Shean of Harvard. However, Dudley, Lawrence, and Shean withdrew.[36] A "Mr. Blaikie," who represented Bennett's interests, protested against allowing Bowie to enter the race, on the grounds that he did not belong to an American College, and was a professional runner. Although his professionalism was admitted, the objection was overruled.[37] So three students only, from Amherst, Cornell, and McGill, competed in the first intercollegiate track event. The Canadian won, with "the roughs shouting in exultation over the success of their fa-

34. *Scottish-American Journal*, September 12, 1872.
35. *Ibid.*
36. *The Cornell Era*, September 12, 1873, p. 2.
37. *Ibid.*, The Report does not state who actually overruled the objection, but the reasons given were that "Canada is generally considered to be a part of America and it was only stipulated that the contestant should be an undergraduate, and although Bowie is a professional runner, he was allowed to enter the race."

vorite, Bowie."[38] Although the result may have been contrary to Bennett's wishes, "the race was a success in every respect,"[39] and he no doubt felt gratified by the enthusiasm shown toward his promotion and encouraged for the future. In fact, more track events were featured the following year, but in the interval two other colleges took up track and field. Neither of these included a two-mile race, however.

In October, 1873, following the complaint that "much has been said, and little done, toward arousing an interest in field sports in college, till this fall," Williams started its field sports, with silver cups as prizes. The events were: putting light weight, standing long jump, running long jump, vaulting with a pole, half-mile race, three-legged race, standing high kick, one-mile footrace, throwing the baseball, and scrub races—a total of ten events.[40] All but the last three were featured at Princeton's Caledonian Games three months earlier.

Two of the events listed were noteworthy, the half-mile and vaulting with a pole. The former did not appear in the Oxford versus Cambridge meeting until 1899, the latter until 1923.[41] They were a part of the few meetings of other Athletic Clubs in England.[42] Pole-vaulting was definitely of Caledonian extraction. It has been stated that it "has not been scientifically practiced so long as other more popular events, but soon after the holding of Caledonian Games in Great Britain began pole-vaulting was added to the programmes,"[43] and also, "more precisely the art of

---

38. *Ibid.*
39. *Ibid.*
40. *The Williams Vidette*, October 18, 1873, pp. 32–33.
41. Abrahams and Bruce-Kerr, pp. 23, 36.
42. Wilkinson, pp. 100–10.
43. Malcolm W. Ford, "Pole-Vaulting," *Outing*, April 1892, p. 42.

pole vaulting was introduced in the United States by Scotch immigrants."[44] George Goldie has been termed "the father of the pole-vault."[45] Certainly the event was participated in by more American than English students, and the event enjoyed a much greater popularity in the United States.

Pennsylvania students also organized an athletic association in the fall of 1873 and held their first meeting, but the contests "merely consisted of throwing the baseball and a running match." Seven events were featured in the spring of 1874, and all matched Princeton's, with the same exception of throwing the baseball.[46] The pole-vault at Williams was this event's first college appearance outside Princeton. Pennsylvania and Yale were also participating in the hop, step, and jump after its debut at Princeton, and this event, also, was indigenous to the Caledonian Games. In England it only "made its first appearance at the AAA Meeting of 1914."[47]

At the Saratoga regatta of 1874, five footraces were featured, a one-mile run, 100 yards, three miles, seven-mile walking race, and 120-yards hurdles.[48] Eight colleges competed, including Columbia, Cornell, Harvard, Princeton, Wesleyan, Williams, and Yale. The former was victorious on the river, six years after George Rives's enthusiastic endorsement from England. This was called the first "really general inter-collegiate athletic contest," and Ben-

---

44. Roberto L. Quercetani, *A World History of Track and Field Athletics, 1864–1964* (London: Oxford University Press, 1964), p. 230.

45. *New York Times*, February 25, 1920, p. 12.

46. George W. Orton, *History of Athletics at Pennsylvania, 1873–1896* (published by the Athletic Association of the University of Pennsylvania), p. 17.

47. Quercetani, p. 258.

48. *New York Herald*, July 15, 1874, p. 6; Krout, p. 188; *The Cornell Era*, September 11, 1874, p. 3.

nett, Jr., was thanked for his "costly prizes."[49] It was
claimed beforehand that the regatta should prove to be
"national in character and as full of general interest as the
Oxford and Cambridge contest is in England."[50] The
American desire for comprehensive interuniversity sport,
such as that enjoyed in England, was always present. But
desire did not necessarily mean duplication. American intercollegiate track and field competition, when it evolved,
was largely a product of environment and local influence.

After Bennett's latest promotion, any students who in-
tended to take up the new sport might have begun with
the five events seen at the regatta and afterwards enthusiastically endorsed by the *Harvard Advocate*.[51] But the
American students did not adopt these events. As an alternative to baseball and boating, the previous athletic activities at Columbia, Pennsylvania, Yale, Williams, and
especially Princeton, were respectable enough and suit-
able for them. Before the next regatta featured even more
foot-races, Harvard, Amherst, and Stevens began field
days for athletic sports. These were similar to their pred-
ecessors elsewhere. All three institutions, for example, included a three-legged race and a half-mile race.

However, the Saratoga appendages provided the element of intercollegiate competition in track events, and
this was Bennett's most significant contribution. Rivalry
was intense between the institutions. The Harvard runner
dropped out halfway through the mile race in 1874, "to
the great delight of the Yale men"; and "this ended the
sports of the Regatta Week at Saratoga—a week marked
by great enthusiasm, unprecedented delays, bitter jeal-

49. *Harvard Advocate*, October 1, 1874, p. 11.
50. *New York Herald*, July 15, 1874, p. 6.
51. *Harvard Advocate*, October 16, 1874, p. 19.

ousies between rival crews, unsatisfactory decisions and general discomfort."[52]

Some institutions saw in the new sport a chance to ease their discomfort. It offered the possibility of greater competitive success than some had achieved in baseball or boating. Also, these new devotees were not unaware of what their rivals had already accomplished in track and field.

An editorial appeared in the *Amherst Student*, written three months after the 1874 regatta, in which the writer acknowledged that athletic sports in America, "now the theme of universal discussion and interest," were probably introduced from England, and then continued to complain that "baseball and boating are about the only athletic sports practised here . . . baseball, boating; boating, baseball, such is at present the narrow limit of our sports." He stated further:

> The Scotch have shown great ingenuity in devising such games, and we can imagine nothing more interesting to the public, or beneficial to the whole college, than the institution of a grand field-day, for the exhibition of skill and strength in such sports under the stimulus of a few small prizes in each department.[53]

Two weeks after this plea came another which indicated the effects of the appendages to the two regattas, and respect for Princeton's George Goldie:

> Two years ago a two-mile foot race was introduced and all of us who were at Springfield can recall the excitement felt as Benton made his sturdy effort. Last year quite a variety of

52. *The Cornell Era*, September 11, 1874, p. 3.
53. *Amherst Student*, October 17, 1874, p. 130.

races was engaged in, and the prospect bids fair that these
minor contests will grow yearly in importance. If Amherst
enters the regatta next year, what can she do in these par-
ticulars? In boating we can hardly hope for the first place
against men who have been training and racing while we
were idle. In Baseball we will do well, as our nine is in
splendid trim. But we can do a great deal for our College by
competing and gaining the victory in these other physical
efforts. We must work through. At present Williams has a
splendid show for all such races. She has her own contests,
and men are trained by these. Princeton has the advantage
of an accomplished athlete at the head of her gymnasium
who, himself, has won many a prize at the annual Scottish
games of the Caledonian Club in Philadelphia. Shall Amherst retire and leave the place to others?[54]

Obviously not; to "do well" was too important, and these
pleas resulted in the first athletic sports at Amherst on
Saturday, November 7, 1874. The events, showing the
Caledonian influence mentioned by the editorial writer,
were: 100 yards, throwing ball at a distance, standing long
jump, running long jump, hop, skip, and jump, three-mile
walking race, throwing ball at a mark, running high jump,
sack race, three-legged race, two-mile race, wrestling, and
a half-mile race.[55] A potato race, wheelbarrow race, hammer throw, quarter-mile, hurdles, football kicking, greased
pig race, fat man's race, and consolation races were added
later in the "Cider Meets" on Blake Field.[56]

Around the time that the Amherst editor pleaded his
cause for the new form of athletic activity, it was also
begun at two other institutions. The first meeting of the

54. *Ibid.*, October 31, 1874, p. 140.
55. *Ibid.*, November 14, 1874, p. 147.
56. *Ibid.*, November 9, 1878, pp. 45–46. Dr. Hitchcock was often
referee at these Cider Meets.

Stevens Athletic Association in October, 1874, was also characterized by great similarity to the Princeton Games of 1873 and 1874. (Even the grand old Scottish term "putting the stone" was used). Other events were: standing long jump, 100 yards, running long jump, hop, skip, and jump, three-legged race, standing high jump, running high jump, mile walk, kicking football, throwing baseball, half-mile run, and consolation races.[57] Ten of these matched Princeton's events.

The poor showing of Harvard men at the Saratoga meet in July, 1874, led to the formation of the Harvard Athletic Association.[58] As elsewhere, this association was formed as an undergraduate club to sponsor track athletics. Like Amherst, a written plea in the student publication preceded the first field meeting:

> The formation of a Harvard Athletic Association is something which has long been needed to develop general athletics among us. We cannot hope to compete successfully with other Colleges until we have held contests among ourselves, both for the improvement of the majority and for the selection of proper representatives. The students should give this new association earnest support, both by joining the club and by entering for the coming games; and ere long Harvard will not be behind hand in these particulars.[59]

The editor of the *Harvard Advocate* in 1874, Benjamin R. Curtis, was the first president of the new association. The events for the first meeting at Jarvis Field, on Saturday, October 24, 1874, were: 100 yards race, running high jump, one mile running race, running long jump, hurdle race,

---

57. *The Eccentric*, March 1875, p. 45.
58. *Class of 1875, Secretary's Report*, No. 1 (Cambridge, Mass., 1875), p. 5.
59. *Harvard Advocate*, October 16, 1874, p. 19.

throwing a baseball, two-mile run, half-mile run, three-legged race, and three-mile walk.[60] Harvard, too, saw possibilities of competitive success in the new sport, and wanted to eradicate the failure of its first attempt in intercollegiate track competition.

Another regatta was due in 1875. Before it took place, there were at least eight colleges where track and field programs had been started: Amherst, Columbia, Harvard, Pennsylvania, Princeton, Stevens, Williams, and Yale. Although the first track running races ever held at Cornell took place in 1873,[61] and its representatives performed well at the regatta footraces in that year and the next, the first full track and field meet did not take place until 1879. This was rather unusual, but the graduation of Cornell's two star runners in 1876 "saw the interest in track forgotten."[62] Which other colleges would also take up track and field in the near future was largely determined by the new sport's affinity with rowing, or, to be more precise, by membership of the Rowing Association of American Colleges.

Obviously, this was not an earlier criterion. Columbia began track and field in 1869, but did not enter intercollegiate competition in rowing until 1873.[63] Although rowing was very popular at Princeton, as already mentioned, it did not join the Rowing Association of American Colleges until 1874, a year after the Caledonian Games were started there.[64] Pennsylvania was not involved in any of

---

60. Copy of the program for the "Harvard Athletic Association, First Field Meeting, Jarvis Field, Saturday afternoon, October 24, 1874," provided by Kimball C. Elkins, Senior Assistant in the Harvard University Archives.
61. Kane, p. 3.
62. Ibid., p. 4.
63. Torney, p. 170.
64. Ibid., p. 174.

the regattas mentioned. It started track and field in 1874, as did Stevens. But the regatta appendages had provided a new form of intercollegiate competition, and a topic of sporting conversation among the undergraduates. Prior to the regatta of 1875, *The Cornell Era* carried this notice:

Athletics at Saratoga

The following circular has been addressed "to the students and Alumni of the several Colleges, constituting the Rowing Association of American Colleges":

The College Athletic Sports will this season be conducted under the auspices of the Saratoga Rowing Association. There will be ten events, eight of which will be open to all the undergraduates of the various Colleges represented in the Grand College Regatta, and two will be open to any and all graduates of said Colleges. The said events will likewise be open to all students or graduates, respectively, of any College or University in the United States, provided that such entry be made by the subscriber by the 4th day of July, next. The games will take place on the day following the Regatta. There will be two sessions. One in the forenoon and one in the afternoon.

The following will be the programme of events:

10 to 12 a.m. Session

1. One mile run
2. One mile walk
3. Three mile run
4. Seven mile walk

3½ to 6 p.m. Session

5. One half mile run
6. Three mile walk
7. 100 yard dash
8. Three mile run
9. 120 yard hurdle
10. Seven mile walk

Numbers 3 and 10, the first three mile run and the second seven mile walk, are events open only to graduate athletes of the several Colleges. The contests will be held at the Glen on a half-mile track, which has changed hands since last season, and is being put in perfect order.

The aggregate value of the prizes will be from two thousand to three thousand dollars. All who intend to participate in these games will confer a favor by reporting as early as possible their names and the number of the events, whether one or more, for which they wish to enter, to W. H. Eustis, Saratoga Springs, N. Y. And all communications relative to the athletic contests, desiring or giving information thereto, may be likewise addressed.

Last year the Foot Races were full of interest. This year the number of events have been doubled, and the gathering together of the athletes from at least fourteen Colleges and Universities, the first in America, representing students by thousands, Alumni of tens of thousands, with their finely developed and faultless physiques, striving each with the other for a goal, animated by a personal pride, as well as by a loyalty to their Alma Mater, will render the contests unusually exciting, reminding one of classic days when national heroes vied with each other and the victor was crowned with an olive wreath.

W. H. Eustis, Committee.

Saratoga Springs, N.Y., May 22, 1875.[65]

Although entry was open to representatives of "any College or University in the United States," because of its circularization, further entries from other members of the Rowing Association of American Colleges were most likely. Before the year of 1875 had ended, four other members of the Association had held their first Athletic Sports Day. All included the three-legged race and, with one possible exception, their programs were again very similar to the Caledonian Games of Princeton. These were

---

65. *The Cornell Era*, May 28, 1875, p. 246.

Dartmouth, Massachusetts Agricultural College, Union, and Wesleyan. Dartmouth's reasons were similar to Amherst's.[66] Again, its program, and those of Massachusetts Agricultural College and Union, would have gladdened the heart of any Caledonian.[67] Wesleyan, however, had only eight events, five of which were the same as the regatta footraces.[68]

Harper's Weekly carried illustrations of the lavish cups to be given as prizes for most events. The winners of the three-mile run and the seven-mile walk received elegant gold watches.[69] Also, "the newspapers ran not several columns, but several complete pages on the land and water Carnival, and the telegraph lines literally hummed as news of the contests was relayed about the country."[70] Admittedly they had a much bigger extravaganza to report, with enough crews competing to necessitate racing in heats. Although there was no collision controversy similar to the Harvard-Yale incident in 1874, more than enough excitement was generated by Cornell's victories and the track events.[71]

An important event took place before the year ended:

On Saturday afternoon, December fourth, a meeting of representatives of ten Colleges was held at the Massasoit House, Springfield. The object of this meeting was to form an Inter-Collegiate Athletic Association. It was deemed

66. John Henry Bartlett, *Dartmouth Athletics* (Concord, N. H.; Republican Press Association, 1893), pp. 68–69.
67. *Ibid.*, pp. 68–69; *The Index*, 1875, pp. 40–41; *College Spectator*, November 1875, p. 6.
68. *The College Argus*, November 6, 1875, p. 34.
69. *Harper's Weekly*, July 24, 1875, pp. 596–97.
70. Torney, p. 183.
71. *Ibid.*, pp. 182–84.

desirable that the Colleges should have direct control of these Inter-Collegiate Athletic Sports.[72]

The Colleges represented were Amherst, Columbia, Cornell, Harvard, Princeton, Trinity, Union, Wesleyan, Williams, and Yale. A constitution was read and adopted, and the sports were placed under the direct management of an elected committee. As a result of this initiative, the First Annual Field Meeting of the Intercollegiate Association of Amateur Athletes of America took place at Glen Mitchell, New York, on July 20 the following year.[73]

The regatta of 1875 had increased some earlier dissension that had appeared in the rowing competition. Brown had withdrawn from the Rowing Association of American Colleges in 1873, to return without success in the two following years. Amherst were not represented in 1874, but placed seventh in 1875. Trinity withdrew permanently in 1874. Bowdoin sent no crews in 1874, and placed only tenth in the University Race of 1875.[74] Although "the magnificence of the College regatta of 1875 far exceeded that of any previous rowing meeting," it represented the Association's final success. Intercollegiate races were again held on Saratoga Lake in 1876, but Amherst, Dartmouth, Trinity, and Yale had already withdrawn and Cornell felt that this would be its last year with the Rowing Association of American Colleges.[75] Also, Harvard had already

---

72. *The College Argus*, December 18, 1875, p. 71. Various sources cite either 1875 or 1876 as the year of the founding of the ICAAAA; but *The College Argus* is the most comprehensive account I have been able to find. Probably several meetings were held in the winter of 1875–76, but this December meeting is certainly important.
73. Frank Presbrey, *Athletics at Princeton: A History* (New York City: Frank Presbrey Co., 1901), p. 404; Krout, p. 188; Leonard and Affleck, p. 283.
74. Torney, pp. 163–64.
75. *Ibid.*, p. 194.

announced her intention to withdraw, but not until after the 1876 race.[76] Harvard and Yale thought the Association "had become unwieldly."[77] When the two oldest inter-collegiate rowing rivals left, it was a great loss to the Association. Only six crews took part that year: Columbia, Cornell, Harvard, Princeton, Union, and Wesleyan. It was recorded that "the College rowing association of the 1870's had risen to great heights, experienced a grand climax in 1875, and then declined with the resounding crash of dissension." The result was the rebirth of dual regatta competition.[78]

Athletic games, on the other hand, were on the rise, and the planning committee that year had succeeded in awakening high general interest in the track athletics.[79] Thirteen events were featured at the regatta of 1876. And "as the expense is comparatively nothing and the training less severe and onerous than for boat racing," reported the *New York Tribune*, "they seem likely to attract a large and steadfast constituency of their own."[80]

The events of the first field meeting of the newly formed Intercollegiate American Amateur Athletic Association in 1876 were: 100 yards, 120 yards hurdles, 440 yards, half-mile, one-mile run, one-mile walk, running high jump, running broad jump, and putting the shot. The 220 yards, pole-vault and throwing the hammer were added in 1877.[81] Not surprisingly, Goldie's pupils felt at home among the events of this first ICAAAA meeting, and Princeton was

76. Blanchard, pp. 66–68.
77. Krout, p. 81.
78. Torney, p. 196.
79. *Ibid.*, p. 195.
80. *New York Tribune*, July 18, 1876, p. 8.
81. *Intercollegiate Association of Amateur Athletes of America* (New York: American Sports Publishing Co., 1928), pp. 112–28.

the winner. It had been agreed that first places would be counted only and in the case of a tie, second places should also count. This system was adopted until 1889–90.[82] The hammer and shot events, particularly, were dominated by Princeton from 1876 to 1879.[83] In fact, the College was described as "facile princeps in athletic games" at this time.[84] This was somewhat flattering, as 1876 was the only time that Princeton ever won the ICAAAA Championship. But the other colleges also were indulging in "Caledonian Games" of their own.

It was the activity of the "Ivy League" colleges which had led to the formation of the Intercollegiate Amateur Athletic Association of America. In fact, the Eastern area of the United States was the center of track and field activity, having the majority of athletic clubs and the site of the meetings, which led to national associations in the sport. But around this time field days were also held at other academic institutions in the United States. The University of North Carolina students held "track meets which consisted of individual jumping and running races" in 1876 and 1877. By 1884, events such as "a greased pig race," "a three-legged race," and "a fat man's race" were included.[85] The Central High School of Philadelphia had its first field day on Saturday, November 11, 1876, which included five events: the 100 yards, standing broad jump, baseball throw, three-mile walk, wrestling, and the 440

---

82. Blanchard, pp. 464–65.

83. *Intercollegiate Athletic Calendar* (Cornell Athletic Board, 1852–1908), p. 23; *Fifty Years of Track Athletics*, ICAAAA Program, Harvard Stadium, May 28–29, 1926, p. 3.

84. "Athletics in America," *Saturday Review*, October 11, 1884, p. 464.

85. Tom Scott, "A History of Intercollegiate Athletics at the University of North Carolina" (D.Ed. dissertation, Columbia University, 1955), pp. 54, 59.

yards. Other events planned "were not contested on account of the rain." The first class meet was held on Washington's Birthday, February 22, 1877, and a mile run, mile walk, and hop, step, and jump were added.[86] Two years later, Marietta College in Ohio held a field day with the following events: half-mile walk, 100 yards, standing and running broad jumps, mile walk, throwing the hammer, mile run, running high jump, standing high jump, standing hop, step, and jump, three-legged race, throwing baseball, hurdle race, two-mile walk, and an "archery match."[87] It was not only in the alma maters of New England and nearby that the Caledonian events appeared in the students' field days.

The English Varsity Meet of 1877 and the American ICAAAA version were significantly different (see Appendix C). Remembering that the Caledonians here also had a fourth of a mile race, a hurdle race, a running long jump, a running high jump, putting the shot, and throwing the hammer long before Oxford and Cambridge began them in 1864, there were also the half-mile, pole-vault, 220 yards, and the one-mile walk. The two former events have been discussed previously. The 220 yards never appeared in the Oxford versus Cambridge match until some time after 1930.[88] Neither did the latter event, which had also been a regular feature of Caledonian Games.

The influence of the Oxford and Cambridge Meets upon American Intercollegiate Track and Field has been exaggerated, at the expense of the contribution of the Cale-

---

86. Franklin Spencer Edmonds, *History of the Central High School of Philadelphia* (Philadelphia: J. B. Lippincott Company, 1902), pp. 254–55.

87. Ralph Clark Patton, "An Analytical Interpretation of the Development of Physical Education and Athletics at Marietta College, Marietta, Ohio" (M.A. thesis, Ohio State University, 1950), pp. 20–21.

88. Abrahams and Bruce-Kerr, pp. 2–41.

donian Games already in the United States. American
students were competing in some events mentioned that
their English undergraduate cousins did not take up for
many years. Also, track and field athletics were in existence in at least five American Colleges before 1874. James
Gordon Bennett, Jr. certainly provided intercollegiate
competition in track races, thoughtfully attached to the
rowing regattas, and thus advertised the new sport in
successful, entrepreneurial fashion. But when it appeared
on the campus in an increasing number of athletic field
days, the programs generally showed the influence of the
Caledonian Games above all.

"The incredible athletic phenomena of the 1870's"[89]
was of the utmost importance in intercollegiate sport.
Events at the end of the 1860s began significant activity.
No doubt track and field athletics would have appeared
in the colleges not too many years after the first Oxford
and Cambridge meeting of 1864, and the New York Athletic Club began in 1868. But the letter from George Rives
to Columbia in 1869, and George Goldie's appointment at
Princeton the same year, helped to accelerate the process.
In the same way, the Harvard versus Oxford Boat Race in
1869 served to increase interest in rowing.

The result was the formation of an intercollegiate sports
association two years later, The Rowing Association of
American Colleges. Victories by Massachusetts Agricultural College (1871) and Amherst (1872) at the Association's annual regattas helped to increase the number of
competing colleges. A writer in *The H Book of Harvard
Athletics* complained, of the period up to 1875, that "the
story of these five years is one consistent record of acci-
dent, confusion, and wasted energy."[90] To be sure, the

---

89. Lucas, p. 50.
90. Blanchard, p. 58.

Association was in decline after 1876 (to be reorganized in 1883), but not before intercollegiate rowing had experienced a glorious heyday and received a handsome national press. Certainly, James Gordon Bennett, Jr. would not have considered his promotion of track races in conjunction with the regattas as wasted energy. These activities suggested the hope of more successful competition in a new sport for the less-able rowing colleges. Like rowing, the sport received some beneficial newspaper and periodical coverage. Unlike the association of the oldest intercollegiate sport, however, the Intercollegiate Association of Amateur Athletes of America, formed in 1875, was of enduring capacity. Once launched it was immediately independent of the sport which had provided its first competitive arena in a limited number of events. In fact, the track events there were relatively unimportant. The colleges adopted track and field events from the Caledonian Games.

6
National Organization of Track and Field and Decline of the Caledonian Games

After the popularity and success of the immediate post-Civil War period, the Caledonian Games entered a period of decline in the latter part of the nineteenth century. The rise of track and field offered a similar alternative to the American competitor and spectator alike, and other sporting amusements appeared to claim the attention of both. Furthermore, the concept of amateur sport was appealing at this time and gained favor. The Scottish character and professionalism of the Games were liabilities against any further progress. As the ethnic custom of a minority immigrant group, they became superfluous to the organization of national American associations in sport. Also, the Caledonian Games were still expensive to produce, but less successful than before, and the smaller clubs particularly experienced financial difficulties. But the athletic Scotsmen, although in decline, justifiably claimed their influence upon the rise of track and field and their position as pioneers of the sport in the United States.

During the 1870s, amateur athletic clubs participating in track and field appeared in many American cities. In 1879, there were about 100 clubs in New York and vicinity.[1] By 1883, there were 150 such clubs in the United States.[2] Part of this growth was owing to the fact that many clubs which had originated for the pursuit of other sports, such as cricket, fencing, gymnastics, or rowing, added track and field athletics to their programs.[3] The New York Athletic Club was a leader in this growth. It held regular athletic meetings and established rules for their conduct, built the first cinder track in the United States, and pioneered the move toward national organization.[4]

The arrival of amateur athletic clubs organizing track and field meetings gave competitors the opportunity to compete in running, jumping, and throwing events outside of the Caledonian Games. The "peculiar" Scottish character of the latter had always set them apart, even at the height of their popularity. While Americans and others could take part in the athletic contests, there were always the bagpipes, the "best-dressed Highlander" competitions, the highland flings and sword-dances, and other exclusive Scottish events to remind "foreigners" of their place. Although it was admitted that "the Caledonian societies participated in athletic games before any of the other clubs," it was also thought that "their games were of a different type from those we have today, and were peculiarly adapted to the participants."[5] Another view was that

1. Robert Korsgaard, "A History of the Amateur Athletic Union of the United States" (Ph.D. dissertation, Columbia University, 1952), pp. 32–33, 50.
2. Albert B. Wegener, *Track and Field Athletics* (New York: A. S. Barnes and Co., 1924), p. 147.
3. Korsgaard, pp. 32–33.
4. John Allen Krout, *Annals of American Sport* 15, *The Pageant of American Series*, 15 vols. (New York: United States Publishers' Association, 1929): 185–89.
5. Augustus Maier, "Physical Training in Athletic Clubs" (thesis, Springfield College, 1904), p. 11.

before the New York Athletic Club was formed in 1868, these same participants "tossed the caber, ran footraces, and drank good Scotch whiskey in honor of Robbie Burns and the domestic affections."[6] Actually, in terms of athletic events, the Caledonian Games were the forerunners of their amateur successors:

> American athletes appropriated the favorite sport of the Scottish immigrants . . . they abandoned some too peculiarly Scottish events like caber-tossing and—more suitable for picnics—the three-legged and sack races.[7]

But even the latter "were sometimes indulged in" by the amateur athletic clubs as late as 1890.[8] And no doubt many American athletes wished they could emulate the successful, if "peculiar," style of Dinnie and Goldie in most of the standard events.

The popular pioneers' Games were not only peculiar, they were professional, which offset their worth.[9] Although they held athletic contests of many types before the amateur clubs did, their professionalism led to a "win at all costs attitude," and there was "constant wrangling betwixt officials and competitors. The officials were incompetent and the athletes were selfish."[10] The Caledonians were actually preceded by other professional runners in the United States, and their foot races and

---

6. Duncan Edwards, "Life at the Athletic Clubs," *Scribner's,* July–December, 1895, p. 4.

7. Rowland Tappan Berthoff, *British Immigrants in Industrial America* (Cambridge: Harvard University, 1953), p. 151.

8. Walter Kershaw, "Athletics In and Around New York," *Harper's Weekly,* June 21, 1890, p. 490.

9. George J. Fisher, "Athletics Outside Educational Institutions," *American Physical Education Review,* June 1907, p. 112.

10. Schroeder, "History of the AAU of the US" (thesis, Springfield College, 1912), p. 2.

walking contests had been common during the first half of the nineteenth century.[11] Pedestrians like John Barlow of England, Thomas Jackson (alias the "American Deer"), George Seward of New Haven, and Louis Bennett (a Seneca Indian known everywhere as "Deerfoot"), provided "goodly wagers" in their time for crowds of thousands.[12] The Caledonian Games, however, provided not only foot races for money prizes, but jumping and throwing events as well. They were a form of professional track and field athletics.

The amateur American track and field meet evolved directly from the Caledonian Games, which "had to compete for public favor with American imitators" in the latter part of the nineteenth century.[13] At this time the concept of amateurism had gained in popularity, national American associations in other sports had already been formed, and new sports appeared to attract the American public. The Caledonian Games found it increasingly difficult to maintain or increase their public favor.

By 1876, it had become common practice for athletic clubs, in their quest for genuine amateurism, to require the positive identification of the athlete, a guarantee of amateur standing, and an entry fee, so that extraneous names would not be included on the program.[14] Two years later, an American Association of Amateur Athletes was formed, but lasted only a few months.[15] But on April 22, 1879, seven clubs became the charter members of The National Association of the Amateur Athletes of America. The clubs were: the New York Athletic Club, Scottish-

11. Krout, p. 186.
12. Ibid., pp. 186–87.
13. Berthoff, p. 151.
14. Korsgaard, p. 37.
15. Ibid., p. 39; Schroeder, pp. 15–16.

American Athletic Club, Manhattan Athletic Club, Staten Island Athletic Club, American Athletic Club, Plainfield Athletic Club, and the Union Athletic Club of Boston.[16] The Association assumed control of the contests for the Amateur Championships of America, and Article IV of the Constitution referred to the events over which the Association claimed jurisdiction:

> The Championship Games shall include:
> Running—100 yards, 220 yards, quarter mile, half-mile, 1 mile, 3 miles.
> Hurdle Races—120 yards, 10 hurdles, 3 ft. 6 ins. high.
> Walking—One mile, three miles, and seven miles.
> Running high jump, running broad jump, pole-leaping.
> Putting the Shot, 16 lbs., throwing the hammer, 16 lbs., throwing the 56 lb. weight.
> Bicycle Race—two miles.
> Individual tug-o-war, tug-o-war, teams of five men.[17]

The Caledonian legacy was apparent. This Association held successful annual championship games, but the spirit of the amateur code had been violated so obviously and so often that in 1885 the definition was revised. In the same year, it clarified its responsibilities further, claiming jurisdiction over "running (all distances), walking (all distances), jumping (of all character), pole-leaping (pole-vaulting), putting the shot, throwing the hammer, throwing of weights, and tugs-o-war (individual and team)."[18] The New York Athletic Club withdrew from the Association in 1886. In spite of this:

in the fall of 1887 it conducted the twelfth annual champion-

---

16. *Ibid.*, p. 47; *Ibid.*, p. 17.
17. Schroeder, p. 24.
18. Korsgaard, p. 50.

ship games. The championship was declared a complete success; the number of entries was the largest ever seen at any games where admissions were charged, excluding the Caledonian Games.[19]

Another critic of the NAAAA, Schuylkill Navy of Philadelphia, wrote to the New York Athletic Club about forming another association. A circular was sent to leading clubs all over the country, and at a meeting held on October 1, 1887, the representatives' efforts "were crowned with success." (Although invited, collegiate associations and clubs declined to attend the meeting, remaining loyal to the NAAAA). The delegates decided that another organization should be formed, and invited other clubs to participate. Their combined activity resulted in the founding of the Amateur Athletic Union of the United States on January 21, 1888. Article XV of its Constitution stated:

JURISDICTION. The Union shall have jurisdiction over the following athletic exercises: 1. Walking (all distances) 2. Running (all distances) 3. Jumping (of any kind) 4. Pole-vaulting 5. Swimming 6. Cross-country running 7. Putting the shot 8. Throwing the hammer 9. Throwing weights 10. Tugs-o-War 11. Boating 12. Boxing 13. Bicycling 14. Bowling 15. Football 16. Lawn Tennis 17. Racquets 18. Skating 19. Fencing 20. Wrestling 21 Gymnastics 22. Quoits 23. Lacrosse.[20]

The concern of the AAU was for all amateur sport and was not confined to track and field. Sports like bicycling

---

19. *Ibid.*, The continual use of the word "games" to describe amateur track and field competition is another aspect of the Caledonian legacy in the United States. In England, they were usually "meetings" or "meets," and the term "games" was usually reserved for team ball-sports.
20. Schroeder, p. 64.

and lawn tennis had attracted many followers. The United States National Lawn Tennis Association had been formed in 1883, and a craze for bicycling arose to supersede all other outdoor activities in the 1880's.[21] A national association had been formed in 1881, and six years later there were over 100,000 confirmed cyclists in the country. Other sports not mentioned in the constitution, like archery and croquet, were also popular.[22] This increase in other sporting amusements also served as a counterattraction to the Caledonian Games, and helped to erode their influence and popularity.

Many of these sports had originated in England, but as far as track and field was concerned, the Caledonian contribution to the formation of the AAU was also acknowledged and undisputed:

> The house of the AAU was literally built upon the bricks of the early pioneers who came from Europe, particularly England, and carried with them their love for sports and games . . . and the athletic-loving Scotchmen who pursued their native games at the Caledonian outings and provided entertainment for more spectators at any single track meet than any other organisation had been able to do until well into the twentieth century.[23]

Between 1879, when the NAAAA had been formed, and 1888, when the AAU began, the Caledonian Games had started to decline. It was proudly declared in 1879 that the Boston Caledonian Club was "the parent and originator of all athletic sports that have not become so popular

---

21. Foster R. Dulles, A History of Recreation: America Learns to Play (New York: Appleton-Century-Crofts, 1965), pp. 182, 193.
22. Ibid., pp. 182–96; Krout, pp. 148–78.
23. Korsgaard, p. 68.

over this continent."[24] In 1885, it was claimed that "finan-
cially the games have been by no means as successful as
those of last year."[25] Some clubs had had large gatherings,
but the amount of money realized was smaller than before.
In some cases a loss was made, the Games "fell quite flat,"
and "at Albany, Hertford, and elsewhere the weather
interfered."[26] Weather was most important to the organizers of the Caledonian Games, for their annual gathering, held outdoors, was their Clubs' main profit-making
concern, and a good day was essential.

Scotsmen doubted, for many reasons, whether the
Scottish Games in the United States could ever again
attain the financial successes of ten years previously. The
main one was that "the novelty has worn off these festivals, similar sports can be seen everywhere at frequent
intervals during the summer."[27] This view was reiterated
eight years later,[28] and in 1896 it was claimed that:

all over the country, during the season, games are held
under the auspices of local athletic clubs, and these games
are nearly all very similar to those which might be witnessed at Hawick or Inverness.[29]

Not only that, but the Scottish rules were "really the basis
on which all athletic contests here are conducted."[30] Scots
had "made Scottish games become the delight of the youth
of America, and the laws they have established for the

24. *Boston Daily Globe*, August 29, 1879, p. 4.
25. *Scottish-American Journal*, September 9, 1885, p. 2.
26. *Ibid.*
27. *Ibid.*
28. *Ibid.*, July 26, 1893, p. 4.
29. Peter Ross, *The Scot in America* (New York: The Raeburn Book
Company, 1896), p. 426.
30. *Ibid.*

guidance of such sports arc generally accepted as the best
as well as the most just that could be framed."[31] The end
result was that the local athletic clubs pushed the Caledonians into the background, largely because their frequent meetings supplied the public demand.[32]

Another reason was that Caledonian records were
regarded with suspicion by "a well-known athletic authority" and others. Judges' returns at the Games, sagging
cross-bars at jumps, and the weight of hammers and
stones, were all in doubt.[33] American track and field, with
its new cinder tracks, spiked shoes, and national association, demanded more meticulous standards. Scotsmen
lamented that:

> Caledonian Clubs introduced such sports into this country
> and their records should be accepted as the standard. But
> it seems they are not.[34]

Their Games had been appropriated, but Scotsmen themselves had contributed to make the process easier.

The Caledonian Clubs had soon concentrated on their
Annual Games, to the detriment or exclusion of other aims
or obligations, and had "been managed as though money-
making were the sole reason for their existence."[35] This
process began when promoters of earlier Games were often
surprised at the crowds which attended them, and the
substantial amount of the gate receipts.[36] The Games be-

---

31. *Ibid.*, p. 429.
32. *Ibid.*, p. 426.
33. *Scottish-American Journal*, August 1, 1888, p. 8; Ross, pp. 426–27.
34. *Scottish-American Journal*, August 1, 1888, p. 8.
35. *Ibid.*, September 9, 1885, p. 2; John L. Wilson, "The Foreign
Element in New York City—4, The Scotch," *Harper's Weekly*, June 28,
1890, p. 513–16; July 5, 1890, p. 522.
36. Ross, p. 426.

came more lavish and expensive productions. Some of the larger clubs, such as Boston and New York, were well able to survive such productions, but many other clubs fell by the wayside in their efforts to emulate them. Even the larger clubs, however, were in a position that was "opposed to all sound business principles" in the face of falling attendances and returns.[37]

It was felt that the only proper course open for the future of the Games was a return to their original and exclusive Scottish character. In recent years, "the pic-nic [sic] features, which used to be so enjoyable have been abandoned," stated the Scottish-American Journal reporter, and "people are getting tired of seeing the everlasting Highland Fling and Sword Dance, to the exclusion of all others." The suggestion was made that the Games be held every two years, with more "mirth-provoking competitions," and a concert or similar entertainment be held in the evening. In short, variety and fun should once again "form the bulk of the sports."[38] These views were repeated before the turn of the century, with other diagnoses for the decline.

The fact that the Games were made open to all comers, and that Englishmen, Germans, Irishmen, Negroes, and others competed in Caledonian Games as well as Scotsmen, was seen as an error of judgment.[39] The answer was to exclude competitors of other nationalities and make the Games Scottish again.[40] Although the Games had waned in popularity, and lost forever their former glory, Scotsmen were encouraged to make the Caledonian Games once again a holiday festival for their countrymen alone in the

37. Scottish-American Journal, September 9, 1885, p. 2.
38. Ibid.
39. Ross, p. 427.
40. Scottish-American Journal, July 26, 1893, p. 4.

United States.[41] No cure for the decline was possible in the nineteenth century, but a return to the traditional, exclusive, and unique past was fervently sought.

The Caledonians had pioneered their athletic sports in their adopted land in the customary professional manner. They had witnessed the adoption of a large number of the Games' events by Americans, under an amateur code. The glorious days of the post-Civil War period were never regained. External forces, and circumstances of their own making, had ushered in new times. These had made the Caledonian Games redundant, except for Scotsmen themselves. But they could take pride in the fact that they had been paid the highest form of flattery.

The appearance of the Scottish Highland Games in the New World in the first place was owing to pride. The exiled Scots' burning nostalgia for his native land was a characteristic which revealed itself in many parts of the world. Like the Highlanders of old, they retained clannish customs thousands of miles away from the heather-clad hills.[42] Without this trait, the Caledonian Games would not have emerged to become the significant influence they were in American sporting history. A famous Scottish author and poet knew his exiled countrymen well:

> Now a wild chorus swells the song:
> Oft have I listen'd, and stood still,
> As it came soften'd up the hill,
> And deemed it the lament of men
> Who languished for their native glen;
> And thought how sad would be the sound,
> On Susquehanna's swampy ground,

41. *Scottish-American Journal*, September 9, 1885, p. 2; July 26, 1893, p. 4; Ross, p. 427.

42. Gordon Donaldson, *The Scots Overseas* (London: Robert Hale, 1966), pp. 201–11.

Kentucky's wood-encumber'd brake,
Or wild Ontario's boundless lake,
Where heart-sick exiles, in the strain,
Recall'd fair Scotland's hills again![43]

---

43. Sir Walter Scott, *Marmion*, canto III, stanza 9.

7
Summary and Conclusions

This study evaluates the influence of the Caledonian Games upon the origin and development of American track and field in the nineteenth century. Like other immigrant nationalities, the Scots established their own cultural associations and societies. One of the customs of which they were fondest was the traditional Highland Games. This was an annual festival, composed of athletic contests, dancing, and music. Most Scottish societies in the United States observed this custom in the second half of the nineteenth century. The majority of these annual gatherings were conducted by the Caledonian Clubs, and the "Caledonian Games" became the prior concern of these clubs.

The first Caledonian Club was organized at Boston in 1853, although Scottish festivals had occurred at least as early as 1836. The New York Caledonian Club was founded in 1856, the Philadelphia Caledonian Club in 1858. Within a dozen years, Caledonian Clubs were a nationwide institution. By the end of the nineteenth century, there were at least 100 such clubs in the United States.

The Caledonian Games became very popular, and crowds of more than 20,000 people were reported. Large gate receipts enabled the Games to become more lavish affairs, increased their importance, and contributed to their proliferation. Originally an exclusive Scottish event, the contests were soon made open to all and other nationalities participated, particularly in the athletic contests. A program usually consisted of 15 to 26 events, chosen from the following: putting the light stone, putting the heavy stone, throwing the light hammer, throwing the heavy hammer, the running high jump, the standing high jump, the running broad jump, the standing broad jump, the hitch and kick, the pole-vault, the hop, step, and jump, the hurdle race, tossing the caber, the short race, the long race, the wheelbarrow race, the sack race, the three-legged race, the broadsword dance, the Highland Fling, boys' hurdle race, throwing the 56-lb. weight, quoits, wrestling, and other novelty events. The Games were professional in nature, and money-prizes were awarded. Valuable gold and silver medals were also given, as well as other prizes.

Amateur track and field began in the United States with the founding of the New York Athletic Club. Members of the New York Caledonian Club successfully competed at this amateur club's first athletic games in 1868. The number of athletic clubs participating in track and field increased rapidly in the next few years. Until a satisfactory definition of an amateur was reached, members of Athletic Clubs and Caledonian Clubs competed at each others' games, and special events were included for this purpose. Individuals from the New York Athletic Club also acted as judges at the New York Caledonian Club's Games.

An outstanding Caledonian athlete and gymnast, George Goldie, was a member of the latter. In 1869, he was appointed Director of the Gymnasium at Princeton. Four years later, Princeton had its own annual version of the Caledonian Games, named in Goldie's honor. In the same year, the first intercollegiate track event was held in the United States. This was a two-mile run, and was won by a Caledonian athlete representing McGill University, Montreal.

The Caledonian Games were also very popular in Canada at this time. In 1867, international games between athletes of both countries were held in New York. Three years later, Caledonian Clubs of the two countries federated as the North American Caledonian Association.

The solitary two-mile race in 1873 resulted from the promotion of James Gordon Bennett, Jr., a sports-minded newspaper editor, and was an addition to the intercollegiate rowing regatta. More races were featured in the next three years. They became popular and attracted the interest of the public and students alike.

Field events were not a part of these promotions. But when the Intercollegiate Association of Amateur Athletes of America was formed in 1876, its first meeting included running, jumping, and throwing events. This was won by Princeton, and the events were similar to Princeton's Caledonian Games. Columbia and Yale had begun athletic field days before 1873, and many other colleges started them between 1873 and 1879. With the exception of Wesleyan, all included running, jumping, and throwing events from the beginning.

American attention had been focused on the interuniversity competitions and the rise of athletics in England about this time. The first Oxford versus Cambridge track and field meeting took place in 1864 with eight events. The programs included only nine events for the next 34 years. This contrasted with the large numbers of various events included in the field days of American colleges. In fact, American students were competing in some events which did not appear in the Oxford versus Cambridge meeting until many years later, some well after the turn of the century. Their field days resembled the Caledonian Games above all.

One of the most successful new amateur athletic clubs in the New York area was the Scottish-American Athletic Club. This was formed in 1875 by younger members of the New York Caledonian Club. It was one of the many clubs involved in the quest for a national amateur association of track and field, which culminated in the formation in 1879 of the National Association of Amateur Athletes of America. Jurisdiction over running, jumping and throwing events was written into the new association's Constitution. Caledonian favorites, such as pole-leaping, throwing the 56-lb. weight, tug-o-war, and others, were included. The NAAAA held championship games which attracted the largest crowd at any American track and field meet, excluding the Caledonian Games.

The New York Athletic Club withdrew from the NAAAA in 1886. Its dissension, and that of other clubs, led to the formation of the Amateur Athletic Union of the United States in 1888. Control over running, jumping, and throwing "of all kinds" was included in its Constitution. It also claimed jurisdiction over many other sports, including bicycling, lawn tennis, and skating. Two authors of histories of the AAU have acknowledged the Caledonian legacy. A famous American athlete and author also wrote of the pioneering of the hammer throw, hop, step, and jump, pole-vault, and shot-put at the Caledonian Games.

George Goldie left Princeton in 1885 to become the first Director of Athletics at the New York Athletic Club. He was very successful at the post for eight years before returning to Princeton in 1893, again as Director of the

Gymnasium. When he died in 1920, his obituary notice in the *New York Times* paid tribute to his pioneering in American athletics, and he was referred to as "the father of the pole-vault."

Scottish regiments held yearly reunions and picnics, at which they celebrated the traditional Games. Other regiments later took part in athletic contests, often using their large armories for this purpose. Many of the participants were members of well-known athletic clubs. Caledonian favorites, such as the three-legged race, wheelbarrow race, and tug-o-war, were also featured in their programs.

By the time the AAU was formed, the Caledonian Games were in decline. Their greatest period was in the 15 to 20 years following the Civil War. Famous athletes from Scotland came over for tours of the Games in the United States. Large delegations of Club members visited other Clubs' Games, and famous people sometimes attended, also.

From 1868 onwards, amateur athletic clubs offered competition in the same running, jumping, and throwing events. They omitted the "peculiar" Scottish events, like tossing the caber and the highland fling, and the elements of Scottish pageantry. Their meetings were frequent, not just annual affairs, and offered an "American" alternative to athletes and spectators. The rise of these athletic clubs reflected the increasingly popular concept of amateurism in sport. The Scottish character and professionalism of the Caledonian Games became an impediment to further progress. Records and judging practices at the Games were criticized, also. Other sports appeared in the 1870s and 1880s to attract the American public. The amateur athletic clubs never matched the consistently large crowds which attended the Caledonian Games.

At this time of falling attendance, some Caledonian

Clubs became too ambitious in their productions and encountered financial difficulties. The larger clubs, like Boston and New York, survived successfully, but the era of the Games' great popularity had gone forever. Scotsmen admitted the fact, and made suggestions for arresting a total decline by reverting to the original, exclusively Scottish festival of the past. They also claimed their rightful position as pioneers of the sport which had become so popular in the United States.

Their claim was a valid one. American track and field emerged from the influence of the early pedestrians, the rise of athletics in England, the appendages at the intercollegiate regattas, and the Caledonian Games. The first attracted large crowds and provided international individual competition in long-distance footraces. It had been customary in America to emulate British sport to a certain extent, and the rise of English athletics did not pass unnoticed. But in the second part of the nineteenth century particularly, the sports of the American people assumed national characteristics. Baseball gradually superseded cricket. The imported version of rugby was transformed into American football. Basketball was invented at Springfield College. When track and field became nationally organized in the United States, it was not merely a replica of English athletics.

The footraces promoted by James Gordon Bennett, Jr. at the intercollegiate regattas provided a new form of intercollegiate competition. Some colleges anticipated a sporting success that they were unable to attain in baseball or rowing. These appendages also attracted the interest of the American public. The colleges' field days, however, also included jumping and throwing events. They bore more resemblance to the Caledonian Games than to the regatta programs, or to the Oxford versus Cambridge meetings in England. The endeavors of George Goldie at Princeton had not passed unnoticed, either.

In fact, the influence of Goldie was a significant individual contribution. He was an expert Caledonian athlete, founder of track and field at the college which won the first ICAAAA meeting, and first Director of Athletics at the New York Athletic Club. As mentioned, he pioneered the pole-vault in the United States. This was one of the many events pioneered by Scottish professional athletes and later adopted by American amateur athletes. The programs of the amateur athletic clubs also included the standing high and broad jumps, hop, step, and jump, throwing the 56-lb. weight, and tugs-of-war. Caledonian novelty events, such as wheelbarrow races, were occasionally featured. Tribute was also paid to the Caledonian origins of hammer-throwing and shot-putting.

The professional athletic contests at the Caledonian Games were the first organized form of track and field in the United States. They were participated in at least 15 years before the founding of the New York Athletic Club in 1868. They appeared all over the country, prospered in a spectacular manner in the post-Civil War period, and then declined with the rise of amateur track and field in the United States and abroad.

The inevitable conclusion is that the sport of track and field athletics in the United States owes much to its Scottish pioneers. Their contribution was too important to be denied, although there were other influences, as indicated. A knowledge of these Games in the nineteenth century, therefore, is essential to an understanding of American track and field history.

Appendixes

APPENDIX A

EVENTS	New York Caledonian Club 1858	New York Caledonian Club 1868	New York Athletic Club 1868	Columbia 1869
1. Putting the Shot	XX	XX	X	
2. Standing Broad Jump		X		X
3. Throwing the Hammer	XX	XX	X	X
4. Running Broad Jump	X	X	X	
5. Running High Jump	X	X	X	
6. Short Race (200–300 yds.)	X	X		
7. Pole-vault		X	X	
8. Standing High Jump	X	X	X	
9. Hop, Step and Jump		X		
10. Hurdle Race		X		X (200 yds.)
11. Three-legged Race		X		X
12. Sack Race	X	X		
13. Wheelbarrow Race	X	X		
14. Hitch and Kick		X		X
15. 1-mile Walk				
16. 2-mile Walk			(PLUS "running and walking contests")	
17. 3-mile Walk				
18. 100 yards				
19. 440 yards				
20. 880 yards			X	
21. 1-mile Run			X	
22. 2-mile Run				
23. 3-mile Run				
24. Throwing Baseball				X (PLUS "150 yards")
25. Kicking Football				
26. Steeplechase				
27. Potato Race				
28. Wrestling				
29. Consolation Race				X

("XX"—denotes "Light" and "Heavy" Hammer or Shot)

Event No.	Yale (May 11) 1872	Princeton (June 21) 1873	Williams (October) 1873	Pennsylvania ("Spring") 1874	Harvard (October 24) 1874
1.	X (1875)	X	XX (1874)		
2.	X	X	XX	X	
3.		X		X	
4.	X	X	X	X	X
5.	X	X			X
6.	X (200 yds.)				
7.		X	X		
8.	X (1873)	X			
9.	X (150 yds.)	X		X	X
10.	X	X		X (120 yds.)	X
11.		X (1874)	X		
12.		X			
13.					
14.	X (1875)	X			
15.			X (1875)		
16.					
17.	X (1873)	X (1874)	X (1875)		X
18.	X (1875)	X	X (1874)		X
19.	X	X	X (1875)		
20.	X (1873)		X		X
21.			X		X
22.					X
23.	X (1875)				
24.	X		X	X (1873)	X
25.					
26.					
27.					
28.					
29.	X				

("XX"—denotes "Light" and "Heavy" Hammer or Shot)

Event No.	Amherst (November 7) 1874	Stevens 1874	Dartmouth ("Fall") 1875	Wesleyan (October 23) 1875	Union (November 2) 1875
1.		X	X		
2.	X	X	X		
3.	X (1878)				X
4.	X	X	X		X
5.	X	X	X		X
6.					
7.			X		X
8.	X (1878)	X	X		
9.	X	X	X		
10.	X (1878)		X (120 yds.)	X (120 yds.)	
11.	X	X	X	X	X
12.	X		X		
13.	X (1878)		X		
14.					
15.		X	X	X	X
16.	X				
17.	X		X	X	
18.		X	X	X	X
19.	X (1878)		X		X
20.	X	X		X	
21.	X (1878)		X		X
22.	X			X	
23.					
24.	X	X	X	X	X
25.		X	X		X
26.					
27.	X (1878)				
28.	X (1878)				
29.	X (1878)	X			

Event No.	Mass. Ag. College 1875	ICAAAA (July 20) 1876	Lehigh (October) 1876	McGill 1876	Brown (December 14) 1878
1.	X	X	X	X	X
2.	X		X	X	X
3.	X	X (1877)	X		X (1879)
4.	X	X	X	X	X
5.	X	X	X		X
6.		220 yds.	220 yds.		
7.		X (1877)	X		
8.	X		X	X	X
9.	X			X	
10.	X (90 yds.)	X (120 yds.)	X (120 yds.)	X (150 yds.)	X (1879)
11.	X		(220 yds.)		X
12.	X			X	X (1879)
13.	X				X
14.			X	X	
15.	X	X	X		
16.			X		
17.			X		
18.	X	X	X	X	X
19.		X	X	X	X (1879)
20.		X	X	X	
21.	X	X	X	X	
22.			X		
23.					
24.	X			(Cricket Ball)	X
25.				X	
26.					
27.					X (1879)
28.	X				
29.	X				

Event No.	Cornell (October 11) 1879	Marietta, Ohio 1879
1.		
2.		X
3.	X	X
4.	X	X
5.	X	X
6.	220 yds.	
7.		
8.		X
9.	X	X
10.		X
11.	X	X
12.	X	
13.		
14.		
15.	X	X
16.		X
17.	X (or Run)	
18.	X	X
19.	X	
20.	X	X (Walk)
21.		X
22.		
23.	X (or Walk)	
24.	X	X
25.	(At Cornell, *cash*	
26.	*prizes* were offered,	
27.	or a medal in lieu,	
28.	"if the contestant	
29.	wished to retain	
	amateur standing")	

N.B. With the exception of the New York Caledonian Club, the dates given refer to the first track and field meeting held by each institution. The sack races and wheelbarrow races usually followed the Caledonian pattern, i.e.; the sacks came right up to the neck, and the contestants in the wheelbarrow races were blindfolded. Also, there were

APPENDIX B

The following entry appeared in the *New York Times* of Wednesday, July 30, 1879, on page 8:

Laying a Corner Stone

The Caledonian Club's New House in Jackson Square

The Caledonian Club laid the corner-stone of a new club-house last evening in Jackson-square, near Eighth Ave., and had a grand parade in connection with the ceremonial. The club was organized in 1856 by a few gentlemen who met at the corner of Varick and Spring streets. It afterward moved into Sullivan St., where it had had its quarters for about 12 years. It has now 500 members, and, therefore, it has been deemed advisable that it should have a building of its own, more commodious than that which it has hitherto occupied. The new Club-house will have a frontage of thirty-three feet and four inches and a depth of eighty-seven feet six inches. It will be four stories high, and will contain a gymnasium, a public-hall, a library, and a parlor. The lot upon which it will stand will cost the club $12,000; about $16,000 will be required for the erection, and the furnishing will cost several thousand more. . . . First the corner-stone was laid by the Chief, M. C. J. Nicholson, and with it was deposited a leaden box, containing various papers of the club, coins of the United States, the daily journals, and such other things as may be supposed to furnish a guiding light to the antiquarian of the future.

Efforts to locate this leaden box in the time available have proved unsuccessful. The museum of the City of New York, The New York Historical Society, and the New York State Historical Association do not have it in their possession. The building which housed the Club was labeled "Chapel of the Comforter" in the *Manhattan Land*

Books of 1934 and 1943, which was taken down sometime between 1943 and 1968. Requests for the date of its demolition to the City Register's Office, 202 Surrogate's Court, 31 Chambers Street, New York, N. Y. 10007, were also unsuccessful.

It is, of course, possible that the leaden box was not removed prior to demolition, in which case it could be anywhere. One hopes, however, that it may ultimately be found, for there is little doubt that its contents would indeed "furnish a guiding light to the antiquarian of the future."

APPENDIX C

1877	1877
23 March. Lillie Bridge	20 July. Glen Mitchell, N. Y.
Oxford v. Cambridge	Second Annual Field
100 yards	Meeting of ICAAAA
440 yards	100 yards
One mile	440 yards
Three miles	One mile
120 yards hurdles	—
Long jump	120 yards hurdles
High Jump	Broad jump
Weight	High jump
Hammer	Putting the shot
	Throwing the hammer
	220 yards*
	Half mile*
	One mile walk*
	Pole vault*

* The half-mile did not appear in the English Varsity Track and Field Match until 1899, the pole-vault in 1923, and the mile-walk and 220 yards are not mentioned at all in the records up to 1930 (see Chapter 3). These four events were featured regularly in Caledonian Games in the United States for at least a decade prior to 1877.

Bibliographical Essay

No thesis or textbook seems to have been solely devoted to the Caledonian Games in nineteenth-century America and their contribution to American track and field athletics. Usually only brief references are to be found, in a variety of works.

A comprehensive account of the Gaelic origins of the Highland Games in Scotland is given in James Logan, *The Scotish* [*sic*] *Gael* (Fifth American Edition, Hartford: S. Andrews and Son, 1851). Other mention of these may be found in *The Scottish Annual and Book of the Braemar Gathering* (Arbroath: The Herald Press, published annually 1924 to date), Wyness Fenton, *Royal Valley: The Story of the Aberdeenshire Dee* (Aberdeen: Alex P. Reid and Sons, 1968), Sir Iain Colquhoun and Hugh Machell, *Highland Gatherings* (London, 1927), and David Webster, *Scottish Highland Games* (Glasgow and London: Collins, 1959). E. Norman Gardiner, *Athletics of the Ancient World* (Oxford: Clarendon Press, 1967), is a classic work on the subject, and other useful information on the Greek Olympic Games is found in John Kiernan and Arthur Daley, *The Story of the Olympic Games, 776 B.C.– 1960 A.D.* (Philadelphia: J. B. Lippincott Company, 1961). An excellent and brief history of the Celts is found in *The Observer* (color supplement), 12 February, 1967. Malcolm W. Ford, in "Hammer-Throwing," *Outing*, September, 1892, and "Shot-Putting," *Outing*, July, 1892, provides brief histories of these events written by an American athlete and author who pays tribute to the Caledonian pioneers of these events. Other brief accounts are found in Roberto L. Quercetani, *A World History of Track and Field Athletics, 1864–1964* (London: Oxford University Press, 1964), and Melvyn Watman, *History of British Athletics* (London: Robert Hale, 1968). Carl Diem, *Weltgeschichte des Sports und der Leibeserziehung* (Stuttgart: J. G. Cotta sche Buchhandbung Nachf., 1960), has a small but interesting section devoted to a history of the Highland Games in Scotland and sports in England. Francis Drake Carnell, *It's An Old Scottish Custom* (London: Peter Davies, 1939), defends in a forthright manner the integrity of the Games as a tourist attraction. The *Scottish-American Journal*, November 21, 1868, gives an account of various Games between 1835 and 1850, held at Edinburgh, Galashiels, Innerleithen, and London.

As general histories of amusements and sports in England, the following are all useful: Horatio Smith, *Festivals, Games and Amusements* (New York: J and J Harper, 1831); Lilly C. Stone, *English Sports and Recreations* (Washington: Folger Shakespeare Library, 1960); Stonehenge, *British Rural Sports* (London: Frederick Warne and Co., 1872); Joseph Strutt, *The Sports and Pastimes of the People of England* (London: Thomas Tegg, 1838); Casper W. Whitney, *A Sporting Pilgrimage* (New York: Harper and Brothers, 1894); and Norman Wymer, *Sport in England: A History of Two Thousand Years of Games and Pastimes* (London: George G. Harrap and Co. Ltd., 1949).

Marcus L. Hansen, *Atlantic Migration 1607–1860* (Cambridge, Mass: Harvard University Press, 1940), provides an excellent analysis of British emigration to North America for over 250 years. Robert Ernst, *Immigrant Life in New York City* (New York: King's Crown Press, Columbia University, 1949), Oscar Handlin, *Boston's Immigrants—A Study in Acculturation* (Cambridge: Harvard University Press, 1959), and Peter Benedict Sheridan, Jr., "The Immigrant in Philadelphia, 1827–1860" (Ph.D. dissertation, Georgetown University, 1957) all give an insight into the cultural activities of immigrants, including the Scots, in large American cities. Thomas D. Clark, *Frontier America* (New York: Charles Scribner's Sons, 1959), briefly mentions the westward expansion of Scottish immigrants. Ralph Henry Gabriel, *The Course of American Democratic Thought* (New York: The Ronald Press Company, 1940), excellently describes the position and contribution of the immigrant in general to American society. Rowland Tappan Berthoff, *British Immigrants in Industrial America* (Cambridge: Harvard University Press, 1953), is the most valuable source of all for material pertaining to the Caledonian Games in nineteenth-century America. Although less than three pages are devoted to this topic, the sources are good and the author gives their documentation. It also provides reasons and statistics for British emigration to America. So, too, does Gordon Donaldson, *The Scots Overseas* (London: Robert Hale, 1966), an excellent reference for Scottish emigration all over the world. For information on the Scotch-Irish, Charles A. Hanna, *The Scotch-Irish*, vol. 2 (New York and London: G. P. Putnam's Sons, 1902), and Henry Jones Ford, *The Scotch-Irish in America* (New York: Peter Smith, 1941), are both useful.

The "First Sportive Meeting" of the Highland Society of New York is described in the *Emigrant and Old Coun-*

tryman, October 19, 1836. Fred Eugene Leonard and George B. Affleck, *History of Physical Education* (Philadelphia: Lea and Febiger, 1947), and Oscar Handlin, *Boston's Immigrants: A Study in Acculturation* (Cambridge: Harvard University Press, 1959), describes the Boston Caledonian Club starting in 1853, but the most informative account of this event is found in the *Boston Daily Globe,* August 29, 1879. R. T. Berthoff, *British Immigrants in Industrial America* (Cambridge: Harvard University Press, 1953), mentions informal sporting activity before 1853. The *Boston Post,* March 18, 1853, and *Boston Daily Evening Transcript,* March 19, 1853, mention "the Seventh Annual Caledonia Ball" in that year. Peter Benedict Sheridan, "The Immigrant in Philadelphia" (Ph.D. dissertation, Georgetown University, 1957), describes a Scots' parade there as early as 1838. Robert Ernst, *Immigrant Life in New York City* (New York: King's Crown Press, Columbia University, 1949), mentions the founding of the New York Caledonian Club in 1856. Two authors of histories of the AAU, Robert Korsgaard, "A History of the Amateur Athletic Union of the United States" (Ph.D. dissertation, Columbia University, 1952), and Schroeder, "History of the AAU of the US" (thesis, Springfield College, 1912), devote their first chapters to the Caledonian Games, and begin with Boston in 1853 and New York in 1856. The former is the more comprehensive account. *The Spirit of the Times,* September 4, 1858, devotes an editorial to the second annual meeting of the New York Caledonian Club, and regularly reports the Games in succeeding years. *The Scottish-American Journal,* published from 1861, regularly published accounts of the Caledonian Games in all parts of the United States, and is an extremely valuable source.

Unfortunately, not many libraries possess issues in any great number. R. T. Berthoff, *British Immigrants in Industrial America* (Cambridge: Harvard University Press, 1953), provides a brief account of the rapid spread of the Caledonian Games to over 100 cities and towns in America.

By the time of the post-Civil War period, the greatest era of the Caledonian Games, references were more frequent and informative. F. E. Leonard and G. B. Affleck, *History of Physical Education* (Philadelphia: Lea and Febiger, 1947), describe it as an especially popular period for the Games. Regular reports and descriptions of the Games in various parts of the country were given in the newspapers and journals of the period, such as the *Boston Daily Globe, New York Times, Scottish-American Journal,* and *Spirit of the Times.* Thomas Wentworth Higginson, "A Day of Scottish Games," *Scribner's,* January 1872, is a detailed account of the Games at Providence, Rhode Island. *Harper's Weekly,* November 2, 1867, describes the New York Caledonian Club's visit to Randall's Island.

All the following are useful for factors affecting the rise of sport in the second part of the nineteenth century in the United States: Frederic L. Paxson, "The Rise of Sport," *Mississippi Valley Historical Review* 4, September, 1917; John L. Krout, "Some Reflections on the Rise of Sport," *Proceedings of the Association of History Teachers of Middle States and Maryland* 26, May 1928; John R. Betts, "The Technological Revolution and the Rise of Sport," *Mississippi Valley Historical Review* 40, September 1953, and "Organized Sport in Industrial America" (Ph.D. dissertation, University of Michigan, 1951); Foster R. Dulles, *A History of Recreation: America Learns to*

Play (New York: Appleton-Century-Crofts, 1965); Max Lerner, *America as a Civilisation* (New York: Simon and Schuster Co., 1957); and Arthur C. Cole, "Our Sporting Grandfathers," *Atlantic Monthly*, July, 1932.

John Allen Krout, *Annals of American Sport* 15, *The Pageant of America Series*, 15 vols. (New York: United States Publishers' Association, 1929), does not mention the Caledonian Games, but otherwise gives a good account of the rise of amateur track and field, with particular reference to the New York Athletic Club. S. Conant Foster, "The New York Athletic Club," *Outing*, September, 1884, gives a detailed account of the latter. For accounts of the rise of amateur athletic clubs and descriptions of their activities, all the following are recommended: Robert Korsgaard, "A History of the Amateur Athletic Union of the United States" (Ph.D. dissertation, Columbia University, 1952); Frederick William Janssen, *A History of American Athletics and Aquatics, 1829–1888* (New York: Outing Co. Ltd., 1888); Augustus Maier, "Physical Training in Athletic Clubs," (thesis, Springfield College, 1904); Charles P. Sawyer, "Amateur Track and Field Athletics," *Scribner's*, June, 1890. The last three authors all mention the Caledonians participating in the New York Athletic Club's first meeting in 1868. Walter Kershaw, "Athletics In and Around New York," *Harper's Weekly*, June 21, 1890, gives a good account of the rise of athletic clubs in the New York area, and he refers to George Goldie's work as Director of Athletics with the New York Athletic Club.

Other material on Goldie is located in Goshua L. Chamberlain, ed., *Universities and Their Sons*, Vol. 2 (Boston: R. Herndon, 1898); Frank Presbrey, *Athletics at Princeton: A History* (New York City: Frank Presbrey Co., (1901); *The Princeton Alumni Weekly*, March 10, 1920;

and Thomas Jefferson Wertenbaker, *Princeton, 1746–1896* (Princeton, N. J.: Princeton University Press, 1946). Dudley Allen Sargent, *An Autobiography* (Philadelphia: Lea and Febiger, 1927), describes his experience working with Goldie in a circus. Besides the information on Goldie, the *Minutes of Meetings of the New York Caledonian Club, 1867–1876,* provides other valuable information, including the Annual Report of the Finance Committee for 1868. The *New York Times,* February 25, 1920, contained Goldie's obituary. Henry Hall, ed., *The Tribune Book of Open Air Sports* (New York: The Tribune Association, 1887), includes an article by Goldie, on Gymnastics. The *American Physical Education Review,* February 1923, shows that Goldie was a charter member of the Society of Directors of Physical Education, founded in 1897. Raymond J. Runkle, "A History of Intercollegiate Gymnastics" (D.Ed. dissertation, Columbia University, 1957), mentions Goldie as promoter of what may have been the first intercollegiate gymnastics meet in the United States.

Gordon Donaldson, *The Scots Overseas* (London: Robert Hale, 1966), describes early Scottish settlement in Canada. Stewart Alexander Davidson, "A History of Sports and Games in Eastern Canada Prior to World War I" (D.Ed. dissertation, Columbia University, 1951), and Henry Roxborough, *One Hundred Not Out: The Story of Nineteenth Century Canadian Sport* (Toronto: The Ryerson Press, 1966), both provide brief, but useful, information on the Caledonian Games in Canada.

David Webster, *Scottish Highland Games* (Glasgow and London: Collins, 1959), is excellent for anecdotes about famous Scottish athletes, and provides much information about Donald Dinnie. R. T. Berthoff, *British Immigrants in Industrial America* (Cambridge: Harvard

University Press, 1953), provides an excellent brief summary of the Games in the United States, in which Dinnie's tour is mentioned. Malcolm W. Ford's "Hammer-Throwing," *Outing*, September, 1892, "Pole-Vaulting," *Outing*, April, 1892, and "Shot-Putting," *Outing*, July, 1892, all concede the Caledonian origins of these three events. The author was one of the most famous American track and field athletes of the time. Robert Korsgaard, "A History of the Amateur Athletic Union of the United States" (Ph.D. dissertation, Columbia University, 1952), also describes the events at the Caledonian Games.

In general, three main sources are useful for determining the first "field day" in various educational institutions: histories of the institutions, histories of athletics in the institutions, and the student publications of the institutions. Since early college sport was administered by the students themselves, the last provide the most detailed accounts. All the following give details relating to early track and field athletics in their respective Colleges: for Columbia, see *The Blue and White*, 2, 1891–92, *The Cap and Gown*, April, 1869, and *Columbia Alumni News*, September 28, 1917. For Yale, see *The College Courant*, March 16, 1872, and May 18, 1872. For Cornell, see *The Cornell Era*, September 12, 1873, and September 11, 1874. For Williams, see *The Williams Vidette*, October 18, 1873. For Harvard, see the *Harvard Advocate*, October 16, 1874, and *Class of 1875, Secretary's Report, No. 1*. For Amherst, see the *Amherst Student*, October 17, 1874, October 31, 1874, November 14, 1874, and November 9, 1878. For Stevens, see *The Eccentric*, March, 1875. For Wesleyan, see *The College Argus*, November 6, 1875, and December 18, 1875. For Massachusetts Agricultural College (now University of Massachusetts), see *The Index*,

1875. For Union, see the *College Spectator*, November, 1875. *The College Argus*, December 18, 1875, gives a useful account of a meeting for founding the ICAAAA. Edwin M. Morris, *The Story of Princeton* (Boston: Little, Brown and Co., 1917), and Franklin Spencer Edmonds, *History of the Central High School of Philadelphia* (Philadelphia: J. B. Lippincott Company, 1902), give details of early athletics at each institution, but more detailed information is usually found in athletic histories of schools and colleges. All the following are valuable: John Henry Bartlett, *Dartmouth Athletics* (Concord, N. H.: Republic Press Association, 1893); John A. Blanchard, ed., *The H Book of Harvard Athletics* (The Harvard Varsity Club, 1923); Robert J. Kane, *Forty Short Years* (Cornell, 1939); George W. Orton, *History of Athletics at Pennsylvania, 1873–1896* (The Athletic Association of the University of Pennsylvania); Ralph Clark Patton, "An Analytical Interpretation of the Development of Physical Education and Athletics at Marietta College, Marietta, Ohio" (M.A. thesis, Ohio State University, 1950); Frank Presbrey, *Athletics at Princeton: A History* (New York: Frank Presbrey Co., 1901); and Tom Scott, "A History of Intercollegiate Athletics at the University of North Carolina" (D.Ed. dissertation, Columbia University, 1955).

For the effects of certain authors on the rise of college athletics from 1850, see Guy M. Lewis, "The Muscular Christianity Movement," *Journal of Health, Physical Education and Recreation*, May, 1966 and John A. Lucas, "A Prelude to the Rise of Sport: Ante-bellum America, 1850–1860," *Quest*, December, 1968. For criticism by two of these authors, see "Why We Get Sick," *Harper's Magazine*, October 1856 and Oliver W. Holmes, "The Autocrat of the Breakfast Table," *Atlantic Monthly*, May 1858. John Rickards Betts, "Sporting Journalism in Nineteenth-Century America," *American Quarterly*, No. 5, Spring, 1953, and William Henry Nugent, "The Sports Section," *American Mercury*, March, 1929, are excellent on early sports reporting in newspapers, and provide material on James Gordon Bennett, Jr. "Athletics in America," *Saturday Review*, October 11, 1884, praises Princeton's athletic ability. *The Cornell Era*, May 28, 1875, carried a circular sent to colleges regarding the track events at Saratoga that year.

John Alfred Torney, "A History of Competitive Rowing in Colleges and Universities of the United States of America" (D.Ed. dissertation, Columbia University, 1958), is an excellent source for information on the regattas of The Rowing Association of American Colleges. Raymond J. Runkle, "A History of Intercollegiate Gymnastics" (D.Ed. dissertation, Columbia University, 1957), mentions the combined gymnastics and track and field "winter exhibitions" at colleges. Edward Mussey Hartwell, *Physical Training in American Colleges and Universities* (Washington: Government Printing Office, 1886), provides excellent information on college gymnasia of the nineteenth century. F. E. Leonard and G. B. Affleck, *History of Physical Education* (Philadelphia: Lea and Febiger, 1947), mention Goldie's appointment to Princeton, the building of the second gymnasium there, and early intercollegiate rowing. H. F. Wilkinson, *Modern Athletics* (London: Frederick Warne and Co., 1868), describes early track and field meets in England, and lists the events. Roberto L. Quercetani, *A World History of Track and Field Athletics, 1864–1964* (London: Oxford University Press, 1964), maintains that the Caledonians introduced pole-vaulting to the United States. Harold M.

Abrahams and J. Bruce-Kerr, in *Oxford versus Cambridge: a Record of Inter-University Contests from 1827–1930* (London: Faber and Faber, Ltd., 1931), list all the events in the Oxford versus Cambridge track and field meets from 1864 to 1930, and is a valuable compilation. Montague Shearman, *Athletics and Football* (London: Longmans, Green and Co., 1889), Albert B. Wegener, *Track and Field Athletics* (New York: A. S. Barnes and Company, 1924), and Caspar W. Whitney, *A Sporting Pilgrimage* (New York: Harper and Brothers, 1894) give interesting accounts of sport in Britain and mention the "picnic events" in the nineteenth century. For an excellent account of the Colonial fairs in America, which included similar events, see Charles M. Andrews, *Colonial Folkways* (New Haven: Yale University Press, 1919). Other good descriptions are found in Carl Bridenbaugh, *Cities in the Wilderness: The First Century of Urban Life in America, 1625–1742* (New York: The Ronald Press, 1938); Edward Eggleston, "Social Life in the Colonies," *Century*, July, 1885; and Sydney George Fisher, *Men, Women and Manners in Colonial Times*, vol. 1 (Philadelphia: J. B. Lippincott, 1898). John Allen Krout, *Annals of American Sport*, vol. 15, *The Pageant of America Series*, 15 vols. (New York: United States Publishers' Association, 1929), does not mention the Caledonian Games at all, but is useful for general information pertaining to the rise of all intercollegiate sport. The *New York Times* and the *Scottish-American Journal* are useful for reports of the Caledonian Games in the 1860s and 1870s. The *New York Herald*, July 15, 1874, compares the American intercollegiate regatta with the Oxford versus Cambridge contest in England; the *New York Tribune*, July 18, 1876, forecasts increasing success for the athletic games. Finally, *Harper's*

Weekly, July 24, 1875, contains a large illustrated account of the 1875 regatta.

Robert Korsgaard, "A History of the Amateur Athletic Union of the United States" (Ph.D. dissertation, Columbia University, 1952), and Schroeder, "History of the AAU of the US" (thesis, Springfield College, 1912), give information about national organizations. The former is the more comprehensive account, particularly on the Caledonians and the rise of amateur athletic clubs, but the latter gives the Articles of the Constitution of the NAAAA and AAU which refer to jurisdiction over athletic events and sports. Albert B. Wegener, *Track and Field Athletics* (New York: A. S. Barnes and Co., 1924), states there were 150 such clubs by 1883. John Allen Krout, *Annals of American Sport*, vol. 15, *The Pageant of America Series*, 15 vols. (New York: United States Publishers' Association, 1929), describes the contribution of the New York Athletic Club well and earlier pedestrian races in America. Augustus Maier, "Physical Training in Athletic Clubs" (thesis, Springfield College, 1904), and Duncan Edwards, "Life at the Athletic Clubs," *Scribner's*, July–December, 1895, both admit the existence of the Caledonian Games before amateur track and field in the United States, but regard them as peculiar and different. Walter Kershaw, "Athletics In and Around New York," *Harper's Weekly*, June 21, 1890, mentions that the amateur athletic clubs also included picnic events in their programs occasionally. George J. Fisher, "Athletics Outside Educational Institutions," *American Physical Education Review*, June, 1907, admits the Caledonian Games' popularity but cannot agree with their professional character.

Rowland Tappan Berthoff, *British Immigrants in In-*

dustrial America (Cambridge: Harvard University Press, 1953), in his brief and lucid account of the rise of the Caledonian Games states that American track and field evolved directly from the Caledonian Games. He does not mention any other possible influences, such as the regatta appendages or the Oxford versus Cambridge meets. Peter Ross, *The Scots in America* (New York: The Raeburn Book Company, 1896), presents a similar argument, but goes into more detail regarding the decline of the Caledonian Games. *The Scottish American Journal,* September 9, 1885, and August 1, 1888, also gives reasons for the decline. Both sources suggest a return to the original, exclusively Scottish character as the remedy.

Foster Rhea Dulles, *A History of Recreation: America Learns to Play* (New York: Appleton-Century-Crofts, 1965), excellently describes all the alternative sporting amusements for the American public in the latter part of the nineteenth century. The *Boston Daily Globe,* August 29, 1879, refers to the Boston Caledonian Club as the originator of the athletic sports which were so popular throughout America. John L. Wilson, "The Foreign Element in New York City—IV, The Scotch," *Harper's Weekly,* June 28, 1890, is a eulogy of Scotsmen in the United States, particularly New York, which also praises the success of the Caledonian Games. Gordon Donaldson, *The Scots Overseas* (London: Robert Hale, 1966), describes the appearance of Scottish associations and societies all over the world, attributed largely to the homesickness of the emigrant. Sir Walter Scott, *Marmion,* canto 3, stanza 9, is a famous Scottish poet's description of that condition.

Index

141

DATE DUE